BTEC First
Diploma in Applied Science

Forensic Science Applications

BTEC First
Diploma in Applied Science
Forensic Science Applications

Writing, editing and production

The **4science** team and associates

*www.**4science**.org.uk*

Images

Photos.com [Jupiter Images]

(unless otherwise stated)

Publisher

Edexcel

190 High Holborn

London WC1V 7BH

United Kingdom

Safety

Teachers should make sure a risk assessment is carried out by a suitably qualified person before students undertake any practical activities.

Printed by Scotprint, Haddington

A catalogue record for this book is available from the British Library

ISBN 9 781846 901966

CONTENTS

☐ = worksheets

☐ = assignments

☐ = essential knowledge and data

Welcome to the BTEC First Diploma in Applied Science: Forensic Science Applications book.

This book has worksheets, to help you learn relevant scientific topics, assignments, to show your progress in this unit and essential knowledge and data, to aid your understanding and help you complete your assignments.

Of course, books can't do everything for you. You still need to work hard to complete your coursework assignments and this will mean finding information from other sources.

During your course induction your tutor will provide you with information (sometimes contained in a student course handbook) about:

- assignment work
- assignment deadlines
- building coursework portfolios
- information gathering
- how you will be assessed
- practical work and health and safety in science laboratories.

More information and help is in the introduction pages of the Core Units book. There you will find a grid where you can track your progress for this and your other units.

The BTEC First Diploma in Applied Science is made up of six units and you must complete the Core Units:

Unit 1: Scientific Principles

Unit 2: Science and the World of Work

Unit 10: Forensic Science Applications will count as one of your other four specialist units.

BTEC courses are known as *work-related* and therefore the assignments you need to complete will have a work-related scenario e.g. identifying hairs as a forensic scientist. Your assignments will usually be broken down into a number of tasks that you must complete. These tasks can be similar to ones that you would do if you were working in that job role e.g. analysing materials from a crime scene.

The BTEC First Diploma course has both unit and course grades. You can achieve a pass, merit or distinction for this unit and for the overall course. If you are successful, the diploma you receive will contain both the unit and course grades. An example of this is below:

The *individual units* have the following grades

Pass for each of two units specified in the course programme

Merit for each of four units specified in the course programme

The *overall grade* for the BTEC First Diploma in Applied Science would be - Merit

---

The *Assessment Evidence Grid*, on the next page, shows:

- the items that your portfolio must contain to achieve a pass grade
- the additional work that you need to include to achieve a merit grade or distinction grade..

Assessment Evidence Grid: Unit 10: Forensic Science Applications

In order to pass this unit, the evidence that you present for assessment needs to demonstrate that you can meet all of the learning outcomes for the unit.

The criteria for a pass grade describe what you must do to pass this unit.

To achieve a pass grade the evidence must show that you are able to:	To achieve a merit grade the evidence must show that, in addition to the pass criteria, you are able to:	To achieve a distinction grade the evidence must show that, in addition to the pass and merit criteria, you are able to:
P1 demonstrate efficient and effective processing of a crime scene and recovery of valid evidence	M1 describe the processing of a crime scene, explaining how the techniques used obtained valid forensic evidence	D1 evaluate the processing of a crime scene, interpreting how the valid evidence collected could be used in a criminal investigation
P2 produce and follow a realistic and achievable plan to analyse two types of biological evidence	M2 describe how well the outcomes met the objectives of the investigation and draw conclusions	D2 justify potential changes to the plans and procedures to improve the conclusions drawn
P3 produce and follow a realistic and achievable plan to analyse two types of physical and chemical data	M3 describe patterns in physical and chemical data and make connections	D3 explain patterns in physical and chemical data and make connections
P4 prepare a statement to give evidence in court identifying the techniques used to obtain the evidence and the conclusions from an investigation	M4 prepare a statement to give evidence in court describing the techniques used to obtain evidence and explain the conclusions drawn from an investigation	D4 prepare a statement to give evidence in court evaluating the techniques used to obtain evidence and justify the conclusions drawn from an investigation
P5 identify the role of the forensic science service within the criminal justice system.	M5 identify the links between the forensic science service and the criminal justice system.	D5 explain the relationship between the forensic science service and the criminal justice system.

WORKSHEETS

ASSIGNMENTS

FORENSIC SCIENTISTS

1: Science and forensics

What do you think it takes to become a forensic scientist?

Work with two or three other students on the two tasks below.

Just make your *best guess*: your ideas don't need to be correct.

Appoint a time keeper and stick to no more than **four minutes** for each task.

Task one

List different kinds of scientific activity you think could contribute to **forensic science**.

Here are two to get you started:

1 medicine, 2 microbiology

_____

_____

Task two

Write your definition of **forensic science**.

_____

_____

_____

_____

_____

Share your ideas

Make sure you have access to:

large sheet of paper (A2 or similar) · computer with Internet access · marker pen(s) and/or printer · scissors and glue · *Blu-Tack* (or other method to display poster) ·

1   Spend 25 minutes researching to check and add to your ideas above.

2   Make a poster to list the **kinds of scientific activity used in forensic science** and a **definition of forensic science**. Go for *good information* and *legible* - don't worry about *neat*!

3   Display your poster for the rest of the class to see.

4   Review the other posters and add to or cross out ideas in your lists above.

5   Write what you think is the best definition of **forensic science**:

_____

_____

_____

_____

Argue it out!

1   Discuss your definitions as a whole class: choose someone to act as a **chairperson** to select who speaks. All comments must be addressed to the chairperson.

2   *Chairperson:*

- Ask someone to read out their definition.

- Check how many people agree. Who has the same or a similar definition?

- Ask someone who disagrees to read out their definition and explain why they think it's better.

3   Continue comparing definitions until no-one has a new definition to suggest.

If necessary, alter your definition on the previous page. You may need to stick some paper over the old definition. As you continue through the unit you may get better ideas. Change your definition whenever you think of a better one.

2:   Case study - DNA detective

Read the following case study. Work with two or three other students to answer the questions. You may need to do some additional research.

Susan Borys is a forensic scientist who analyses DNA evidence for the Royal Canadian Mounted Police. She says:

"I always knew that I would go into forensics and that I was destined to work in a lab. I love the excitement of it, the detective work and the evolving technology."

She likes to watch forensics in TV programmes like *CSI:Crime Scene Investigation:*

"They get some things right but a lot of it is way off, like it doesn't take them any time at all to do the analysis. We laugh about it at work."

Susan Borys has worked on a number of important cases for the Canadian police, including the Swiss Air Flight 111 disaster:

"My role was in matching known samples from family members to those of the victims. We identified all of the victims in 104 days."

Most recently (2002-2007), she has been involved in analysing DNA for the Picton case. Features of the trial include

- February 2002: Picton is arrested and charged with murder
- January 2007: trial by jury begins
- Picton is charged with the murders of six women
- DNA from 30 women has been identified from samples taken from his pig farm
- DNA from three other women has been isolated, but they have not been identified
- The farm has been excavated and demolished, with more than 600 000 pieces of evidence removed

1   Why does Susan enjoy her work?

_____

_____

2   What work, other than crime investigations, does she do?

_____

3   How is it possible to use DNA to identify victims of crime or disasters?

_____

_____

4   When collecting evidence from a scene, why is it important to
     (a)   avoid contamination?

     _____

     (b)   label items carefully?

     _____

3: Fact or fiction?

How do you know the telly got it right? As you learn more about forensic science you will be able to tell.

Each time you see forensics on TV, when reading a book or at the cinema, critically assess what goes on. Is there more fiction than fact? Tell you teacher about it!

You can check by looking things up:

•   Try to find some good websites. For example:

     -    www.forensic.gov.uk

•   Get a textbook. For example:

     -    Pete Moore, 2004,The Forensics Handbook, Eye Books

     -    Richard Platt, 2003, Crime Scene, Dorling Kindersley

     -    N E Genge,2004, The Forensic Casebook, Ebury Press

     -    D P Lyle, 2004, Forensics for Dummies, Lifestyles Paperback [American].

4: Safe working

Wherever scientists work - in the field or in the lab - they encounter many hazards.

They must observe strict safety precautions to maintain their own safety and the safety of others. They also have to meet legal requirements.

Work with two or three other students to answer the following questions. You may need to do some research to find some of the answers.

1   What do these initials stand for:

     (a)   **HSE**   _____

     (b)   **PPE**   _____

     (c)   **COSHH** _____

2   Complete the following:

(a)   **A hazard is ...**

_____

_____

_____

(b)   **A risk is ...**

_____

_____

_____

Safety in the field

Describe _two_ hazards that might be found by Scene of Crime Officers (SOCOs) at each of the following:

An explosion

•   _____

•   _____

A traffic accident

•   _____

•   _____

An earthquake

•   _____

•   _____

Safety in the laboratory

1   What is meant by _sharps_?

_____

2   Describe the precautions you take in your lab when using _sharps_.

_____

_____

_____

_____

_____

sharps bin

3   Hazards from contaminated surroundings can enter and harm the body in a variety of ways. Action can be taken to reduce the risk of harm. Look at the boxes (next page). Draw lines to connect the hazards to the actions that reduce the risk.

method of entry into the body	nature of hazard		action to reduce risk
inhalation	airborne e.g. dusts, smoke, vapours, gases		Use equipment such as spectacles, safety glasses, gloves and other protective clothing.
skin absorption	contaminants that can make contact with the skin e.g. corrosive chemicals		Exercise caution when handling sharp objects. Wear gloves at all times. Dispose of sharp objects in special containers.
ingestion	contaminants that are able to enter the mouth e.g. toxic chemicals		Ventilation and/or respiratory protection (masks).
injection	contaminants associated with sharp objects (such as broken glass or needles) that can puncture the skin e.g. infected blood in hypodermic needles		Wash hands before eating or smoking. Do not bring food into unsuitable areas.

Choose one of the following scenarios:

• Watch a TV or video programme which shows crime scene investigators at work. This may be real life documentary or fictional (e.g. *Waking the Dead*, *CSI*).

• Read a case study of a crime scene investigation e.g. in a book, newspaper or magazine article.

• Investigate a mock-up of a crime scene.

List three hazards that you or the investigators encounter. For each hazard, describe the associated risk *and* the action that you would recommend to reduce the risk.

Hazard 1: _____

Risk

_____

_____

_____

Action to reduce risk

_____

_____

_____

Hazard 2: _____

Risk

_____

_____

_____

Action to reduce risk

_____

_____

_____

Hazard 3: _____

Risk

_____

_____

_____

Action to reduce risk

_____

_____

_____

5: Using new chemicals

When forensic scientists work with a new chemical, they need to find out if it is hazardous. If it is, they carry out a risk assessment. The law (CHIP3) requires suppliers to provide safety information. You will also have information (e.g. HAZCARDS) available in your lab.

DPX is a solution which can be used to mount specimens on microscope slides. Later, you may have the opportunity to use DPX to mount hairs for microscopic inspection. Work with two or three other students to carry out research on _DPX mountant_.

Use one of these websites (or other websites, catalogues or hazard databases as directed by your teacher):

- http://chemdat.merck.de/mda/uk/index.html (type **DPX** in the _Quick search for Merck Products_ box)
- http://www.sigmaaldrich.com/catalog/search/ProductDetail?) (type **DPX mountant** in the _Product name_ box and click the blue lines in the _Safety_ section to go to hazard codes, and safety and risk statements).

What is used to make DPX?

_____

_____

Complete the following.

DPX mountant

Hazard (how harm may be caused)	**Precautions to be taken**
_____	_____
_____	_____
_____	_____
_____	_____

CRIME SCENE INVESTIGATION

1: The scene

The scene of a crime may be where the crime is committed. But if you're a forensic scientist, the crime scene is *anywhere that evidence can be collected*.

Sometimes it's a small area. For example, a murderer, victim and weapon might be found in the same room. In a fraud case, it could be as tiny as a laptop.

But it could be huge. It might start with the shop where the criminal buys the weapon and lead to the route taken as the criminal flees from one country to another.

- You may have seen American TV programmes like *CSI: Crime Scene Investigation*. In America, scientists who visit crime scenes to collect evidence are called **criminalists**. What are they called in the UK?

  _____

- Sometimes forensic scientists show there has been *no* crime. Suggest a situation where a crime may be suspected but none has occurred.

  _____

2: Evidence

There may have been no witnesses, but forensic scientists may be able to find the evidence to convict the criminal. Evidence left at the scene of a crime is sometimes called the **silent witness**.

The five main stages in processing evidence are shown jumbled up (below).

Number them in the correct order.

You can find different types of evidence in crime scenes.

You need to use special techniques.

You must work carefully to provide valid evidence in a court of law.

stage of processing evidence	number
exhibition in court	
initial examination, recording and collection	
laboratory examination, identification and recording	
discovery and recognition of item	
packaging, transport and storage	

Establishing the evidence

You may need to carry out some research to do this work.

Crimes

Quickly, list four or five different crimes:

_____

_____

_____

_____

_____

_____

Types of evidence

Work with one or two others.

- Compare your lists.

- Choose one crime from them and write the name of the crime in the table.

- Complete the table by noting the kinds of evidence that might be obtained from the crime scene, victim or suspect in each case.

- Compare your types of evidence with other groups. If you get more ideas, add them to your table.

the crime: _____

possible evidence		
from crime scene	from victim	from suspects

Special techniques

A wide variety of special techniques are used to find, recover and record evidence. You see these in films and TV programmes, both British and American.

Think about types of evidence that can be found at a crime scene. Take five minutes to list possible techniques that could be used by Scene of Crime Officers (SOCOs):

_____

_____

_____

_____

_____

_____

_____

_____

_____

_____

_____

_____

_____

**From the FBI website
http://phoenix.fbi.gov/pxert.htm**

FBI Phoenix has two Evidence Response Teams (ERT) comprised of Special Agents and Professional Support employees in Phoenix and Tucson. Each member of the ERT receives specialised training in the areas of crime scene management and investigation and in the area of evidence collection and processing.

The ERT is charged with conducting thorough crime scene investigations, performing specialised searches, and serving as liaison between FBI Phoenix and the FBI's Laboratory. When an FBI case requires a complex crime scene search or the use of a specialised forensic technique, members of the ERT are immediately deployed.

Compare lists with other students. Add to yours.

Valid evidence

If evidence isn't collected and recorded correctly, it may not be valid.

* Explain what's meant by *valid evidence:*

_____

_____

_____

_____

* Describe two general procedures you must follow when collecting evidence, to ensure its validity.

_____

_____

_____

_____

3: The first responder

Work with one or two others to answer these questions.

At a crime scene, who is the *first responder*?

_____

_____

_____

As a first responder, you would have a number of priorities:

1 **To ensure safety**

Whose safety is most important? Why?

_____

_____

_____

_____

2 **To give emergency first aid**

What precautions would you need to take to preserve evidence?

_____

_____

_____

_____

3 **To detain and remove any suspect**

How would you do this?

_____

_____

_____

_____

4 **To prevent contamination of the crime scene**

How would you do this?

_____

_____

_____

_____

5   **To record and preserve evidence that may be destroyed or lost**
    Give an example of how you might do this.

_____

_____

_____

_____

6   **To locate and separate witnesses**
    Why are witnesses separated?

_____

_____

_____

_____

7   **To take field notes to record your observations**
    Suggest some things you should record.

_____

_____

_____

_____

4: Initial assessment

Before making a full search for evidence, notes are made at the scene. This is the *initial assessment*.
Give three reasons why it's done.

1 _____

2 _____

3 _____

Sometimes the initial assessment shows that specialists are needed. This may be at the scene or to analyse
the evidence. Give reasons why a SOCO might ask for:

divers _____

dogs _____

an odontologist _____

an entomologist _____

5: Photography

Modern scene of crime investigators use a lot of photography.

Give three reasons why.

1 _____

2 _____

3 _____

6: The collection of evidence

Evidence is found, collected and transferred to the forensic laboratory for further analysis.

Anti-contamination

Describe three methods used by SOCOs to avoid contamination of the crime scene and the evidence that they collect.

- _____
  _____

- _____
  _____

- _____
  _____

Word search

Find 12 items that a SOCO would take to a crime scene (across and down).

Match each item against its use in the table (next page).

Some words may be used more than once.

M	T	S	D	F	S	W	A	B	S	H
F	A	M	U	O	B	L	G	N	D	J
S	P	K	S	R	M	T	O	R	C	H
K	E	B	T	C	A	N	S	Y	A	W
G	L	O	V	E	S	P	H	Q	M	Z
M	Y	X	G	P	K	P	A	P	E	R
N	L	E	V	S	B	V	W	Y	R	T
G	X	S	K	E	T	C	H	P	A	D
E	N	V	E	L	O	P	E	S	Q	O

item	use
	to record the scene and where evidence is found
	to protect evidence for removal
	to make fingerprints visible
	to pick up evidence without contaminating it
	to collect fluid samples
	to help to see small objects
	to prevent contamination by the investigator
	to mark off the crime scene

7: The chain of continuity

Careful record keeping is essential to maintain a **chain of continuity** from crime scene to court. Why is it important that the chain isn't broken?

_____

_____

Every bit of evidence is labelled carefully. Records are kept to show the chain of continuity. With one or two other students, decide what you need to record, to maintain the chain. Then design a label for the evidence containers to record the information you need. Stick a copy in this space.

Some forensic authorities prefer not to use labels, but write directly onto evidence or containers. Give a reason for this.

_____

Standard procedure: Making a paper packet for trace evidence

You will need

clean sheet of A4 paper • standard envelope

Small items and trace evidence like hairs, fibres or paint fragments can be placed into a clean piece of paper, folded securely and sealed in an envelope. The pharmacy fold (also called a **bindle**) is often used.

Method

1 Fold the paper as shown, right.

2 Put your bindle into the envelope and save it for later.

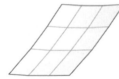

1 crease by folding into thirds in both directions

2 fold over lengthways

3 turn up bottom third

4 open end to form a pocket (material may be placed in here)

5 fold over top third and tuck into bottom flap

6 seal with tape (do this later)

Reconstructing a crime scene

Your class will work in small groups to make posters to represent different crime scenes.

Later, you will look at other people's posters and try to work out what happened.

You will then take part in a class discussion on your observations and findings.

For your group's poster:

1 Choose a crime or a suspicious event. You could use ideas from real crimes reported in the media or fictional crimes from TV, films or books. Or you could make up your own.

2 Make notes to create a crime scene scenario by:

- choosing a self-contained area, e.g. a room, building, street or field

- making up a series of events that take place when the crime is committed.

3 Sketch out the area on your poster.

4 Draw or stick pictures or other items on your poster to represent:

- the key features found in the area (for example a room would include furniture)

- evidence of what might have happened or what might link the criminal to the scene.

Do not use any labels or text - they could give the game away!

5 Provide clues:

- that a crime took place

- that show what the crime was

- for evidence that helps identify the criminal

- for evidence of what happened at the crime scene.

6 Display your poster for the other groups to look at.

How exactly you put your poster together is up to you - but you must work to the deadline set by your teacher. Items on the poster do not need to be realistic!

Look at the posters from other groups that are on display.

From each poster, try to work out what happened.

Use your observations of the poster to help you to complete a table like the one below. Your teacher will give you spare copies for each poster that you evaluate. Make suggestions of possibilities if you're unsure or the evidence is not clear.

questions	decision	evidence/reasons
has a crime been committed?		
what was the crime?		
how was the crime committed?		
what other events took place at the scene?		
what might link a criminal to the scene?		
what might link a criminal to the victim?		

Class discussion

Compare your decisions with others. For each poster:

- Do you agree with other groups?
- When could you form definite conclusions?
- When did you need more evidence?
- What sort of evidence would help you to be more certain?
- Were decisions in line with the scenario devised by the group who made the poster?

After your discussion, complete these statements.

The most useful types of evidence were _____

_____

Disagreements occurred when _____

_____

HAIR AND FINGERPRINTS

1: Biological trace evidence

Individuals vary from one another in many ways, so biological materials can often provide evidence to link suspects to crime scenes or to victims. Some of these may be sources of DNA.

Discuss and write answers to these questions with another student.

List three types of biological traces that can be found at crime scenes.

1 _____   2 _____   3 _____

Insects can also provide useful evidence. What information can forensic scientists obtain by studying insects?

_____

_____

Why do forensic scientists collect trace evidence, like hairs, when it's not as conclusive as DNA profiling?

_____

_____

SOCOs must not contaminate a crime scene or collected evidence with their own hairs or hairs from other sources on their clothing. How can they prevent such contamination?

_____

_____

> 'As a rule, said Holmes, the more bizarre a thing is, the less mysterious it proves to be. It is your commonplace, featureless crimes which are really puzzling, just as a commonplace face is the most difficult to identify.' **Arthur Conan Doyle**

2: Fibres and hairs

Fibres

You will be given a garment, or part of a garment, to inspect and sample for hairs and fibres. It will be provided in a clean plastic bag. You should work in a thoroughly clean area (if necessary, clean the bench before you start). Wear protective clothing to prevent contamination with your own hairs or fibres. Inspect as much of the garment as you can in the time available.

Standard procedure: Collecting hairs and fibres

Health and safety

A risk assessment must be carried out before starting work.

You will need

forceps • clean sheet of paper and an envelope (x2) • clear adhesive tape • scissors • acetate sheet • protective clothing e.g. hood, goggles, surgical gloves • garment (or piece of fabric) • fine permanent marker pen • torch (optional) • small piece of absorbent paper e.g. filter paper

Note: You should be familiar with the use of a light (optical) microscope to carry out this procedure.

Method

1   Fold the paper to form a small open-ended packet (this is called a **bindle**, see instructions in *Crime scene investigation, Standard procedure: Making a paper packet for trace evidence*).

2   Place the garment in a clean, well lit area.

3   Use a magnifying glass or hand lens to carefully inspect the garment using a **linear search routine** (see *Essential knowledge and data* section).

4   If available, use a torch or lamp to illuminate the area you are inspecting.

5   Use forceps to remove any visible hairs or free fibres and place them into the bindle.

6   Fold over the end of the bindle and seal with tape.

7   Label the envelope with your **name**, **date**, **time** and **the location the garment was taken from**. Add a **reference number**: unless told otherwise, use your initials and numbers in sequence for each new piece of evidence that you label.

8   Store as instructed for a later assignment.

9   Cut a piece of clear adhesive tape about 10 cm long.

10   Press firmly onto the surface of the fabric and peel away. Inspect - if any small pieces of hair or fibres are present, stick it down onto a piece of acetate sheet.

11   Take two or three more samples using this method.

12   Use a permanent marker to label the acetate and place into an envelope; label and seal as before.

Hairs

With luck, similar hairs from a crime scene and a suspect can be found and matched. But even hairs from the same source can vary. Normally a sample of at least 25 hairs is taken to establish the *norm* for a person or animal - but you won't have time to do this! Use hairs provided or that you collect.

External structure of human hair, showing scales of cuticle

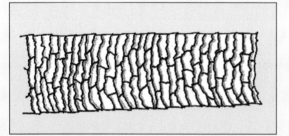

Standard procedure: Using a light microscope to compare hair samples

Health and safety

A risk assessment must be carried out before starting work. Wear protective clothing and eye protection. DPX contains xylene (dimethylbenzene) [HARMFUL].

You will need

hair samples • microscope • slides and coverslips • teat pipette • forceps • contact adhesive • mountant such as DPX or clear nail varnish • fine permanent marker pen • lightweight protective gloves

Method: Making a dry mount

1   Wash your hands. Handle the slide and coverslip by the edges to avoid fingerprints.

2   If using a self-illuminated microscope, use a blue filter (if possible) to counter the yellowness of the tungsten filament lamp.

3   Label a slide with reference number of sample, using a permanent marker pen.

4   Label the sample packet with date, time, your name and purpose of removal.

5   Open your sample packet and carefully open the bindle.

6   Place 2 drops of adhesive about 5 mm apart in the centre of the slide.

7   Use forceps to remove a hair from the sample and glue it in place.

8   Note the colour of the hair and if it is straight, wavy or curly.

9   Make sure the ends will lie under the cover slip, if necessary fold the hair.

10 Add a cover slip and press it down onto the adhesive.

11 Examine under low power, then x100. Look for:

  •   the scales of the cuticle

  •   the tip

  •   the root.

  Note: not all of these may be visible or present.

12 Use the table of observations (next page) to record the features you can see.

Method: Making a wet mount

1   Either ...

  •   Use a teat pipette to add DPX [CARE - HARMFUL, IRRITANT] or other mountant at the edge of the cover slip. It should be drawn under by surface tension.

  •   If too many bubbles form, touch a piece of absorbent paper to the edge of the cover slip and add more mountant fluid to the opposite edge - it should be drawn through towards the paper.

  •   If this fails, remove the cover slip and place fluid directly over the hair. Replace the cover slip by lowering at an angle to squeeze air over to one side. Remove any excess mountant with absorbent paper.

  Or ...

  •   Place a drop of clear nail varnish in the middle of a slide.

  •   Place a new hair from the same source as before onto the varnish.

  •   Add a cover slip, dropping it gently down at a slight angle to push air to one side.

  •   Push down so the varnish reaches the edges of the cover slip.

Types of medulla

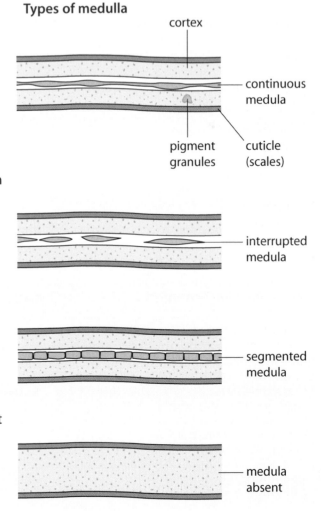

cortex

continuous medula

pigment granules

cuticle (scales)

interrupted medula

segmented medula

medula absent

2   View using low power first.

3   A mountant like DPX has the same refractive index as hair. So it has a similar effect on light as the hair, making it easier to see the medulla, if present. Scan along the hair looking for the medulla.

4   Note in the table of observations whether the medulla is absent, continuous, fragmented (different size gaps) or segmented (regular sized gaps).

5   Note the thickness of the medulla. Is it less than or greater than half the thickness of the hair, or absent?

6   Look for:

- the scales of the cuticle
- pigment granules
- ovoid bodies
- air spaces
- the tip - is it tapered, rounded, split, cut?

Record your results in the table of observations, below.

7   Repeat for at least one reference hair taken from the comb of a suspect.

8   **Optional:** If you have a digital camera which can be connected to a microscope, obtain images of hairs for comparison, using the same types of mount, magnification and illumination. If you have time, use appropriate software to crop and rotate images so that they can be lined up side by side for comparison. This simulates the use of a comparison microscope. Print and staple copies to this page.

Observations (continues on next page)

specimen reference number		shape		colour	
type of mount	DRY			WET	
cuticle (scales small or large, flat or raised)					
medulla structure and size (less than 1/3 of diameter or more than 1/2 of diameter)					
other features (describe)					

specimen reference number		shape		colour	
type of mount	DRY			WET	
cuticle (scales small or large, flat or raised)					
medulla structure and size (less than 1/3 of diameter or more than 1/2 of diameter)					
other features (describe)					

specimen reference number		shape		colour	
type of mount	DRY			WET	
cuticle (scales small or large, flat or raised)					
medulla structure and size (less than 1/3 of diameter or more than 1/2 of diameter)					
other features (describe)					

specimen reference number		shape		colour	
type of mount	DRY			WET	
cuticle (scales small or large, flat or raised)					
medulla structure and size (less than 1/3 of diameter or more than 1/2 of diameter)					
other features (describe)					

Conclusions

Write a conclusion in the space below. Do you consider that any of the hairs you have looked at are from

• the same person

• an animal?

Justify your decisions.

_____

_____

_____

_____

_____

What would you need to do if your sample was to be used as evidence in court?

_____

_____

_____

_____

Comparing hairs

In America, a scientist published research suggesting that, if enough similarities between two hairs were found, a unique match was possible. Hair evidence became very important in many cases. The FBI carried out research to show that 11% of hairs matched by experts were actually from different people. Many cases have been re-opened and DNA evidence has been used to prove the innocence of people falsely convicted on the basis of hair evidence alone.

How could the FBI show that hairs were from different people?

_____

_____

How is it possible for hairs from different people to be matched as identical?

_____

_____

Not everyone thinks that hair comparison is useful or valid.

Mark Webster of the Forensic Science Consultancy says:

'The trick with hair comparison is not to worry about using a comparison microscope. Use the flip of a coin instead, it's much cheaper, easy to use both in the field and lab, and actually rather more accurate.'

(http://www.truthinjustice.org/hair.htm)

Kathy Steck-Flynn, who teaches forensics, says:

'The chances of a single hair from a victim being found on a suspect might be 1/800 that it got there accidentally. If, however, hair from a suspect is also found on the victim the probability of an accidental transfer increases to 1/640 000. Hair should be used as support to other evidence.'

(http://www.truthinjustice.org/hair.htm)

Write a brief explanation of your opinion of hairs as evidence.

Do you think they can be useful or would it be better not to use them?

_____

_____

_____

_____

_____

3: Fingerprints

In 1948, June Devaney was taken from her hospital cot and battered to death. Fingerprints from a bottle failed to match medical staff or known criminals held on file. Every male voter in Blackburn was contacted and fingerprinted, but none of the 40 000 sets matched. The police were able to locate 200 unregistered men and this time they found a match. Peter Griffiths confessed and was hanged. The fingerprints of the others were publicly destroyed.

Work with one or two other students to answer these questions. You may need to do some research.

What are the three basic patterns found in fingerprints?

1 _____   2 _____   3 _____

Explain why it is important to have a classification system for fingerprints.

_____

_____

The **Henry** system worked well for identifying criminals who were using aliases, but it was not much use for matching fingerprints found at crime scenes. Find out and explain why.

_____

The UK National Automatic Fingerprint Identification System (NAFIS) contains about 6.5 million prints.

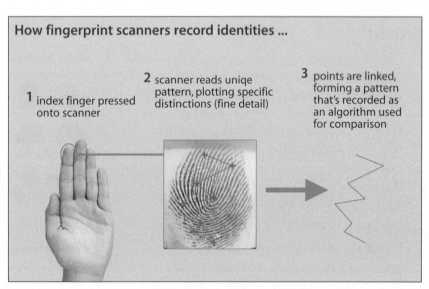

How fingerprint scanners record identities ...

1 index finger pressed onto scanner

2 scanner reads uniqe pattern, plotting specific distinctions (fine detail)

3 points are linked, forming a pattern that's recorded as an algorithm used for comparison

- In the future, passports will require fingerprints. These will be scanned and added to the national database.

- A scheme is being trialled which allows roadside digital scanning of finger prints of motorists stopped by the police. It takes about 15 minutes to check someone against the database to confirm their identity.

Describe some of the advantages of having a computerised system for fingerprint identification.

_____

_____

Do you think that the proposed expansion of NAFIS is mainly (a) an infringement of civil liberties or (b) a major step forward in the fight against crime? Explain your answer.

_____

_____

_____

_____

4: A fingerprint investigation

Your task is to match fingerprints from a *crime scene* with those in a database. Your manual search will give you an insight into how such systems work. However, modern databases scan and digitally encode fingerprints for automatic identification.

Work in a group of three or four. You will each record a set of your fingerprints in a database and then leave *crime scene* fingerprints on a glass beaker. You will then swap with another group and attempt to match each *suspect* to a beaker.

Make a database of fingerprints

Health and safety

A risk assessment must be carried out before starting work.

You will need

finger print ink in pad or with white tile and ink roller • fingerprint record sheet • white self-adhesive labels • hand washing facilities • paper towels

Method

1. Collect the materials. Your teacher will provide you with standard fingerprint forms. If you use the FBI style of form, you will need to record 10 *rolled* prints taken of each finger, one at a time. This is followed by 10 *slapped* prints taken simultaneously in the space underneath.

2. Wash and dry your hands thoroughly. If your fingertips are wrinkled, rub in some moisturising lotion, but wipe off the excess.

3. Choose an alias - your criminal name.

4. Take it in turns to act as the Fingerprint Officer. The Fingerprint Officer should write your criminal name and the date in the correct places on the form.

5. Prepare the ink. If using a tube of ink, place a small blob about 2 mm in diameter on the centre of a white tile. Use the roller to spread the ink thinly and evenly by repeatedly rotating through 90°.

6. Practise making fingerprints on scrap paper. Place the finger side down and roll gently from one side to the other on the inkpad or inked tile. Check there is an even layer of ink on the finger.

7. Repeat the rolling movement to transfer a print onto paper, so the finger ends up facing in the opposite direction. Note:

    •   only very light pressure is needed
    •   place the paper on a bench rather than a table, so the arm is raised almost horizontal
    •   remove the fingers *up and away* to avoid smudging.

8. Check a clear print has been obtained. If necessary, wipe off or add more ink to the finger.

9. When you're satisfied with your technique, make rolled prints in each section of the form.

10. Finish by placing all four fingers of each hand down at the same time to make the *slapped* or flat prints, with no rolling movement. Then record the thumbs. Check that at least one of the two prints (rolled or slapped) for each finger is clear.

11. If fingerprints have to be repeated, either use a new form or cover a poor print with a white self-adhesive label.

12. Use the slapped prints to check that the rolled prints have been recorded correctly.

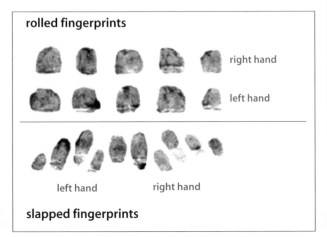

rolled fingerprints

right hand

left hand

left hand   right hand

slapped fingerprints

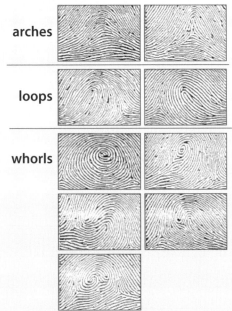

arches

loops

whorls

13 The Fingerprint Officer and the *criminal* should sign the form as correct.

14 Carry out an initial analysis by identifying the basic pattern of each print as arch (a), loop (l) or whorl (w). Record the pattern in this format, on the fingerprint form.

You've now classified your fingerprints. Record this at the top right hand corner of the fingerprint form. Everyone should then make a datasheet like this, to include everyone in your group:

name	date	officer	signature	database code
Fingers Malloy	12/04/07	R. Symmonds	*RSymmonds*	1 4 0 0 4 1

Making *crime scene* fingerprints

Health and safety

A risk assessment must be carried out before starting work.

You will need

gloves • clean glass or beaker • fingerprint database (record sheets)

Method

One member of your group should leave *incriminating* fingerprints on a separate glass or beaker.

1 One person should use a glove or cloth to collect a clean glass or beaker.

2 Choose one person to act as the criminal:

• rub the fingers and thumb of one hand over your forehead or nose

• grasp the glass or beaker firmly with the ends of your fingers and thumb to form *latent* fingerprints

• release without smudging.

3 The evidence should now be handled carefully to avoid smudging or adding fingerprints. Swap beakers and fingerprint record sheets with another group.

Matching fingerprints to the database

Health and safety

A risk assessment must be carried out before starting work. Wear protective clothing and eye protection. Avoid breathing dust.

You will need

gloves • clean glass or beaker • clean microscope slides • beakers with fingerprints from *crime scene* • fingerprint database (record sheets) • clear adhesive tape • scissors • white and dark card (or acetate sheet and OHP) • magnifying glass or hand lens • digital camera (if available) • fine carbon or iron powder or cocoa with container • talcum powder • fine permanent marker pen • soft brush

You now need to provide evidence to link the culprit to the scene of the crime, by matching the fingerprints on the glass to the fingerprint database. You first need to practise developing latent prints.

Method: Making latent finger prints to develop

1   Rub a forefinger on your forehead or the side of your nose and press it gently but firmly to make latent fingerprints at both ends of a clean microscope slide.

2   Use the method below to practise developing the fingerprints, using a dark powder at one end of the slide and the white talcum powder at the other.

     Which powder do you think will give the better results? _____

3   If you need to improve your technique, try again with new slides.

4   Use the method to locate and develop as many fingerprints as you can on the *evidence* beaker.

Method: Dusting a non-porous surface to develop latent fingerprints

1   Place a large sheet of clean paper or newspaper on the bench to collect stray powder.

2   Put on gloves.

3   Collect a small amount of the powder to be used (e.g. in a small beaker). Choose one which will give good contrast.

4   Inspect the surface to be tested for signs of prints and support it horizontally.

5   Dip a clean brush into the powder and gently shake the excess back into the container.

6   Hold the brush just above the surface and twirl or tap gently to distribute powder over the test area.

7   Very lightly, draw the brush over the surface of the glass to reveal the prints.

8   Tap the brush over the container to remove as much powder as possible.

9   Very gently, brush surplus powder from the prints until they are clear. Avoid over-brushing which could smudge the prints.

Method: Lifting developed fingerprints

1   Carefully press adhesive tape over each print. Avoid smudging and make complete contact without air bubbles or gaps.

2   Lift and stick onto card that gives a good contrast or onto acetate sheet for using an overhead projector to magnify the image.

3   Label by writing across the card/actetate and tape (to prevent tampering with the evidence).

Using fingerprints as evidence

1   From their positions, try to identify which hand and which finger each print or partial print comes from.

2   Use a marker pen to give each print a unique code and, if possible, photograph them.

3   If hand and fingers are identified, you can include **R** or **L** for right or left, **F** = fore, **M** = middle, **R** = ring and **L** = little. (How can you recognise which hand has been used?)

4   You will need at least one good clear print.

5   Use the database to track down the suspects:

- First compare your evidence with the datasheet classification code. Use the information from the fingerprints you have been able to develop.

- You can match or eliminate to come up with a final shortlist for making a more detailed examination. *Fingers Malloy* (see page 25) has no whorls on his right hand, so if any right hand whorls are found on a beaker, they can be eliminated.

- Put a tick or cross against each individual.

6   Write the *names* of your shortlist here (it could already be down to one person or you may not have been able to eliminate anyone). Explain how you came to your decision.

_____

_____

_____

_____

7   Now make a direct comparison between the lifted fingerprints and the fingerprint record sheets of your shortlist. If you have lifted prints onto acetate, you can project them to enlarge them.

8   Note the features your suspect's fingerprints have in common with your evidence fingerprints.

9   When you believe you've got a perfect match, choose one good fingerprint for comparison. On a photograph of the print, label five features that match the fingerprint in the database. If no photograph is available, use labelled sketches to record your points of comparison. Staple your photo or diagram to this page.

10   If you were to appear as the expert witness in court, what key point would you make to link the suspect to the scene of the crime?

_____

_____

_____

_____

_____

11   Return the fingerprint records to the other group and check your identification. Write the *criminal's* name here and indicate if the identification was correct or false.

Owner of fingerprints identified as: _____

Verified as correct: **YES/NO**

12   If your identification was incorrect, explain why.

_____

_____

5: Optional activities

Your teacher may ask you to try these.

- Try to use a digital scanner to obtain fingerprints. Use the associated software to enhance and store the images (for example, change contrast or enlarge).

- Create a computer database of classified fingerprint records. Use the database to search for matching fingerprints found at a mock-up of a crime scene.

BODY FLUIDS AND DNA

1: Body fluids

SOCOs look carefully for bloodstains at the scene of a crime. These can provide evidence concerning not only the perpetrator, but also of the crime itself. After careful recording, a simple presumptive field test is carried out to establish if a stain is likely to be blood. Samples sent to the lab can then be more carefully analysed.

How could the bloodstains at the scene be recorded?

_____

What is meant by a presumptive test?

2: Is it blood?

Investigating stains for blood

Two simple tests rely on the presence of a peroxidase enzyme (catalase) in the blood:

- luminol gives a bright pale blue luminescent compound that glows in the dark
- colourless phenolphthalein indicator in Kastle-Meyer reagent is turned pink.

The tests are not conclusive, because some other substances contain peroxidase enzymes and can cause a positive result. However, the tests are cheap and can be conducted in the field. Samples can then be taken for further testing in the lab, for example for blood typing or DNA profiling.

Your task is to compare these two tests. Use the following standard procedure to test the stains on pieces of cotton cloth or white paper towel.

Standard procedure: Testing for blood

Health and safety: A risk assessment should be carried out before starting any procedure. Phenolphthalein, blood [BIOHAZARD] - dispose of safely. Wear protective clothing, gloves and eye protection. Ethanol [HIGHLY FLAMMABLE] - work away from naked flames.

You will need

3% hydrogen peroxide • Kastle-Meyer reagent • Luminol solution in spray bottle • teat pipette • forceps • filter paper • distilled water • various numbered samples of stains on white cotton or white paper towel • pencil • darkroom

Method: Kastle-Meyer test

1   Use a pencil to label a piece of filter paper to match the sample to be tested.
2   Moisten the filter paper with distilled water.
3   Touch the stain to be tested to transfer some of the substance to the filter paper.
4   Add two drops of Kastle-Meyer reagent.
5   Add two drops of 3% hydrogen peroxide.
6   A pink colour indicates the likely presence of blood.

Method: Luminol test

1   Spray each numbered sample with a small amount of Luminol solution (avoid breathing droplets).

2   Inspect in darkness.

3   A bright, pale blue glow indicates the likely presence of blood.

Results

Record your results in this table and indicate if the tests agreed or not.

sample	Kastle-Meyer pink colour (✔or✗)	Luminol pale blue glow in dark (✔or✗)	test agree (✔) or disagree (✗)
1			
2			
3			
4			
5			

Questions

1   Suggest possible explanations for any differences.

_____

_____

_____

2   A forensic scientist would use other clues to decide if a stain was blood or not. Which sample(s) do you think is (are) most likely to be blood? Explain your decisions.

_____

_____

_____

3   Which samples that gave a positive result do you suspect are not blood? In each case, explain what makes you think this.

_____

_____

_____

4   Various fresh plant and animal tissues will give positive results, but not if they have been cooked. Explain why.

_____

_____

_____

3: Collecting blood

SOCOs must make sure that collection and storage techniques avoid contamination of a blood sample and cross-contamination with other samples.

Carry out the following procedure on a sample stain.

Standard procedure: Collecting a blood sample for further analysis

Health and safety: A risk assessment must be carried out before starting any procedure. Wear protective clothing, eye protection and gloves

You will need

forceps • sterile cotton (gauze or fabric) • clean, A4 paper • clean envelope • clean scalpel • distilled water • plastic containers (optional)

Method

1 If it's possible to transport and store it, remove the entire stain with the item/surface it's on, or cut away a sample.

   • If analysis is to be carried out within two hours, place in a sealable plastic bag or bottle.

   • If sample is to be stored before analysis, air dry thoroughly. Do not expose to bright sunlight. Wrap in clean paper, seal with tape and place in an envelope.

2 Label containers with: **name of collector**, **date**, **time**, **reference number** and **location sample was taken from**.

3 If blood has to be removed from a surface:

   For liquid blood

   • Use forceps and clean sterile cotton gauze or fabric to soak up a sample. Treat as in step 1, above.

   • If blood has started to dry, moisten the cotton gauze with distilled water.

   For dry blood

   • Use a clean scalpel or other suitable tool to scrape dried blood onto a clean sheet of paper. Fold and place in an envelope.

4 All samples must be stored and labelled separately.

5 Refrigerate or freeze samples as soon as possible.

6 Carry out further analysis as soon as possible. Whenever possible, retain some of the original sample in case further tests are needed.

Results

Record the information you write on your evidence label.

_____

_____

_____

_____

_____

_____

4: Blood typing

Human blood can be classified as groups **A**, **B**, **AB** or **O** depending on the presence or absence of antigens **A** and **B** on the surface of the red blood cells. Your task is to follow instructions to test a blood sample using anti-A and anti-B blood sera. You may be allowed to test your own blood or use artificial blood.

Mixing red blood cells with an anti-serum that contains antibodies for any antigen present causes them to stick together in clumps. This reaction is **agglutination**. This is different to the clotting action of the blood, which involves sticky threads of the protein fibrin.

You may also be able to test for the presence of the Rhesus factor. Agglutination with anti-Rh antibody indicates Rh+ (Rhesus positive) blood. No agglutination is Rh-(Rhesus negative).

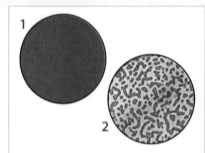

1 antibody does not affect red blood cells

2 agglutination due to antibody/antigen match

Standard procedure: Blood typing for the ABO system

Health and safety: A risk assessment must be carried out before starting any procedure. Blood [BIOHAZARD] - dispose of safely (see point 2 of the method).

You will need

blood testing kit • white dropping tile • teat pipettes • blood sample • wax pencil or permanent marker pen • sterile toothpicks • disinfectant •

Method

1   **Either** follow instructions that you're given by your teacher, **or** use the method below.

2   If testing your own blood, use only your own and dispose of lancets and waste in disinfectant as instructed.

3   Label one well in the dropping tile as anti-A and another at least one space away, as anti-B.

4   If using anti-Rh, label another well accordingly.

5   Place testing tile on a paper towel to absorb any spills.

6   Add the appropriate anti-sera to each well, being careful to avoid contamination.

7   Add one drop of blood to each anti-serum. (If using your own blood, carefully follow the instructions that you are given.)

8   Mix the contents of each well carefully with a separate clean toothpick.

9   If using real blood, dispose of the toothpicks in disinfectant.

10 If agglutination occurs, the samples will appear speckled. Sometimes real blood clots and will form large clumps - ignore this.

11 Record your results below.

12 If testing more than one blood sample, stick a copy of your own table over this section.

Results

anti -A agglutinates? (✔or✗)	anti -B agglutinates? (✔or✗)	anti Rh (if used) agglutinates? (✔or✗)	blood group of sample =
			_____

Question

1   On average, what are the chances that this sample will be a different group to another sample taken at random? You will need to look up the proportion of each blood group in the population.

_____

5: DNA

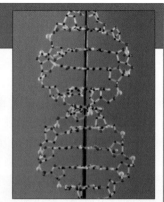

You will need to do some research to answer the questions in this section. Work with another person and ask other pairs for help if you get stuck.

DNA profiling is a very reliable method for matching numerous crime scene samples to individuals. It can also be used to show that samples *do not* belong to *innocent* suspects.

Questions

1   What is DNA short for?

_____

2   Why do some experts dislike the term DNA fingerprinting?

_____

3   Many biological traces left at crime scenes or on victims of crime are potential sources of DNA. Circle the traces that are potential sources of DNA for forensic analysis.

skin cells • hair roots • epithelial (lining) cells in urine • red blood cells •

cheek cells in saliva • muscle tissue • tooth enamel • sperm

4   What cell organelle is found in all samples that can be used as sources of DNA for DNA profiling?

_____

5   What part of a DNA molecule forms the genetic code?

_____

Extracting DNA

DNA must be extracted before it can be analysed. You will now investigate the basic principles of the process by extracting a large sample of DNA from onion tissue.

Extraction of DNA from onion tissue

Health and safety: A risk assessment must be carried out before starting any procedure. Cut away from fingers. Ethanol is highly flammable.

You will need

10 cm³ measuring cylinder • beaker • test tube • rubber bung • own-brand *value* washing up liquid (detergent) • salt • distilled water • onion • kitchen knife • chopping board • food processor/blender • balance (measuring to 1g) • filter paper • filter funnel • ethanol [HIGHLY FLAMMABLE] • kitchen knife [CARE]

Method

1 Mix 10 cm^3 of washing up liquid with 3 g of salt and 100 cm^3 water in a beaker.

2 Cut an onion into chunks and weigh out 100 g.

3 Place the washing up mixture with the onion into the blender. Liquidise for about five seconds, until the onion is well broken up.

4 Filter the mixture into a beaker.

5 Half fill a test tube with the filtrate.

6 Add an equal volume of ethanol, not quite to the top.

7 Close the end of the test tube with a bung and invert three or four times.

8 DNA should appear as a cloudy white solid.

Questions

1 Why was a food processor/blender used?

_____

2 What was the purpose of the detergent (washing up liquid)?

_____

3 What precautions would you need to take if you were preparing a sample for DNA profiling?

_____

_____

6: DNA profiling

A number of technical terms are used by DNA analysts.

Match the terms to the correct descriptions. One has been done for you.

Terms	Descriptions
electrophoresis	the process that *amplifies* a small DNA sample into a large one
restriction enzymes	are pieces cut from a DNA molecule for the old method of profiling
primers	cut DNA into pieces
fluorescent dyes	are small pieces of DNA
PCR	the process that separates DNA pieces
RFLPs	The national DNA database
STRs	mark the start and stop points for DNA replication
SGM+	allow pieces of DNA to be located during electrophoresis
NDNAD	name of the system used to profile DNA

Modern DNA profiling in the UK uses the SGM+ or Second Generation Multiplex Plus system.

- What is *multiplexed* in the process?

_____

- Using the SGM+ system, what are the odds that two people will share the same DNA profile?

_____

Kary Mullis got a bonus of $10 000 for inventing PCR. Later his company sold the patent for $300 million! PCR allows a great amplification of even tiny traces of DNA, as little as 10 picograms.

How many picograms make a gram?

_____

Why does this pose a problem for the SOCOs?

_____

_____

- The National DNA Database contains more than three million DNA profiles. But 40 000 samples of DNA taken from crime scenes have not been matched. Why is this?

_____

- Expert testimony is important in court to establish connections *beyond reasonable doubt*. Why is DNA evidence not considered to be proof?

_____

Impact of DNA profiling on crime detection in the UK (2004/2005)

crime	overall detection rate / %	detection rate when DNA crime scene samples are used / %
all recorded crime	26	40
domestic burglary	16	41
vehicle theft	15	24
theft from vehicle	8	63
criminal damage	14	51

- Which crime showed the greatest increase in detection rates?

_____

- Which crime showed the least increase in detection rates?

_____

- Explain this difference in improvement in detection rates.

_____

Marion Crofts was raped and murdered in 1981. Microscope slides were deliberately stored for nearly 20 years until more sensitive DNA profiling tests were developed. In 1999 the DNA LCN technique was used to convict Tony Jasinskyj.

What does LCN stand for?

_____

What property of DNA makes it possible to produce DNA profiles starting from tiny amounts of DNA?

_____

_____

Which process is used to increase the amount of DNA for profiling?

_____

7: Faking DNA

Cunning criminals sometimes use DNA profiling to their advantage.

Dr Sneeburger was accused of assault by female patients. The police took blood samples for DNA analysis on a number of occasions, but no match was obtained. It later emerged that he had surgically implanted a device to give samples of someone else's blood.

Suggest another way in which criminals might fake DNA evidence.

_____

_____

_____

_____

_____

_____

1: Evidence from entomology

Alton Coleman was a brutal criminal who went on a savage crime spree in 1984. When captured, he was wanted for eight murders, seven rapes and fourteen armed robberies.

In one case he had befriended a woman and abducted and murdered her nine year old daughter, Vernita. When the body was found in a derelict building three weeks later, it was in an advanced state of decay. The bathroom door was removed and taken to the lab, where one of Coleman's fingerprints was found.

1   What stage of decay would Vernita's body have reached?

_____

2   Give three examples of evidence that may have been used to identify Vernita's body.

   1   _____

   2   _____

   3   _____

3   Why wouldn't the fingerprint on its own have been enough to convict Coleman?

_____

Coleman had witnesses who saw him with Vernita on the afternoon she disappeared and alone the following morning at 8 o'clock. The FBI sent the insects and pupae found with the corpse to forensic entomologist Bernard Greenberg. They wanted him to give them a time of death.

Blowflies can be useful in estimating the PMI (post mortem interval) - the time since death occurred. They usually lay eggs on the corpse after two days. If forensic entomologists find a maggot at the early third instar stage on a corpse (taking local conditions into account) they may work out that this stage will appear about eight days after eggs are laid.

4   What would they estimate for the PMI?

   _____

   _____

5   Why was it going to be difficult for Greenberg to establish the time of Vernita's death, using blowflies?

   _____

   _____

   _____

   _____

the blowfly life cycle has six parts: the egg, three larval stages, the pupa and adult

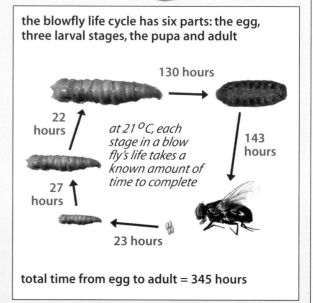

130 hours

22 hours

at 21 °C, each stage in a blow fly's life takes a known amount of time to complete

143 hours

27 hours

23 hours

total time from egg to adult = 345 hours

Greenberg carefully incubated the pupae he had been sent. Black blowflies emerged, then sheep blowflies. Eventually, bluebottles appeared. Greenberg knew that, at a constant 15 °C, bluebottles take 33 days from egg to adult. But at that time of year, temperatures in Illinois average about 25 °C during the day and seldom fall below 16 °C at night.

6   Did Greenberg expect the bluebottles to have taken more or less than 33 days to complete their life cycle?

_____

Greenberg turned to agricultural entomologists for help. These scientists advise farmers on pest control, including choosing the best time to spray a crop with pesticides. They use *accumulated degree hours* to calculate the stage reached. Time elapsed in hours is multiplied by temperature in °C. Hence an insect kept at 150 hours at a constant 20 °C will take 100 hours at 30 °C to reach the same stage.

7   How long would this insect take to reach the same stage at 15 °C?

_____

8   At 21 °C, blowfly larvae take 23 hours to hatch from newly laid eggs. How long would it take them to hatch at 30 °C?

_____

9   What other information did Greenberg need, to help estimate the time when Vernita died?

_____

Greenberg then set about making more than 700 calculations using reports from weather stations near the crime scene. The evidence suggested Vernita died at about midnight, May 30. He knew this could not be *completely* accurate, but he also knew that bluebottles are not active at night. This meant it was likely that the eggs were laid early the next morning.

Could you act as an expert witness and convince a jury? Greenberg did. Coleman was found guilty and sentenced to death. But another state got there first. He was executed on 26th April 2002 for another murder committed in Ohio.

10   Why was Greenberg's evidence important to convict Coleman?

_____

2: Evidence from odontology

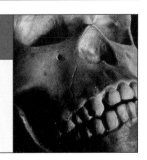

The mummified remains of a woman were found in the disused cellar of a hotel in Australia. A forensic odontologist was able to determine her age to within 12 months. The Missing Persons Bureau were then able to suggest a name and the odontologist was able to confirm her identity within 48 hours of the body being found.

Questions

1   In what field is an **odontologist** an expert?

_____

2   Suggest how the odontologist was able to:

•   give an age for the victim

_____

_____

•   confirm her identity.

_____

_____

3:   Evidence from anthropology

Forensic anthropologists may be asked to produce a profile of a person using skeletal remains.

Your task is to determine which parts of the skeleton can be used to estimate height.

Estimating height from parts of the skeleton

You will need

plain A4 paper • A4 graph paper • tape measure •
optional: computer and spreadsheet program

Method

Work with a partner and share your results with two other pairs. Both draw a large *matchstick* person on a sheet of A4. Try to get all the proportions correct. Include feet and hands, and mark the positions of the elbows and knees with small circles.

Compare your sketches. Do they look the same? Save them for later. You will now measure real people to see if your drawings were in the correct proportions ...

1   Use this table to record your results or, if you can, use a spreadsheet.

person and sex (M/F)	length / cm						
	height	arm span	ulna	hand	femur	foot	head
1							
2							
3							
4							
5							
6							

2   Start by measuring height and arm span. Height should be with feet flat on the floor and without shoes. Arm span is from fingertip to fingertip with the arms stretched out horizontally.

3   Complete the table using your measurements and those from two other pairs. Length of hand is from the wrist joint to the end of the middle finger. You will need to move your leg to try to locate the top of the femur.

4   Plot graphs (using spreadsheet software if possible) of each dimension against height. Start each axis scale from zero. If doing it by hand, plot three graphs each.

5   Plot a graph of *length of ulna* against *length of foot*.

6   Where you have a clear linear (straight line) relationship, rule lines of best fit between the points, starting from the origin.

7   Find the slope for each straight line drawn. As the line passes through the origin (0,0), choose a (high) value from the horizontal axis and divide it into the corresponding value from the vertical axis.

8   Which parts of the skeleton can be used to estimate height? Give the multiplication factor needed in each case.

part of skeleton	multiplication factor to give height

Questions

1   If you were working as a forensic anthropologist, would you feel confident if asked to use bones to give an estimate of the height of a person? Explain your answer.

_____

_____

_____

_____

_____

2   What relationship did you find between the length of the ulna (forearm) and the length of the foot?

_____

_____

3   Draw another *matchstick* person on a sheet of A4. Use your findings to get all the proportions correct.

4   Search the internet for a picture of Leonardo Da Vinci's drawing, *Proportional Study of Man in the Manner of Vitruvius*. Do you agree with the proportions?

_____

_____

4: Investigating victim identification

When the head of John Hayes was found in a London dock in 1726, it was washed, the hair was combed and it was set up on a post in the hope that passers by might recognise the victim. At the time there were no forensic scientists. There wasn't even a police force. Today, there are many experts and techniques to help identify the victims of crime or disasters.

Your task is to work with a partner to carry out some research. You will write two short reports to explain how a forensic anthropologist and an odontologist can help identify human remains.

- Use the table to make a list of techniques that could be used in victim identification.

anthropologist	odontologist

- Work together to make a shortlist of two techniques for each type of scientist that you will investigate further. Underline or highlight them in your table above.

- Choose which scientist you will research. Toss a coin if you are undecided.

- Write a short account (no more than 150 words) for each technique to explain what it involves and how it can be used to identify human remains. Use any format you like, including illustrations as you think appropriate.

  - Create your reports in a form which can be displayed for the rest of the class to read.

  - If possible, word process your account.

- Check your reports with your partner to make sure they are clear.

- Display your reports for the rest of the class to see. If they have been word processed, they could be transmitted through a discussion forum.

- Compare your accounts with others. Don't just look for information; see which styles and formats communicate the information best.

Disaster Victim Identification

Three very reliable methods for disaster victim identification are **fingerprinting**, **odontology** and **DNA profiling**. Surprisingly, **visual identification** is the least reliable. Describe one problem that can arise for each method:

fingerprinting _____

_____

odontology _____

_____

DNA profiling _____

_____

visual identification _____

_____

1: Investigating the chemical and physical analysis of evidence

In this section you will

- learn how to use some methods of analysis employed by forensic scientists
- do some research to find out how they work and how they are used.

This will allow you to develop the skills that you need to complete the assessment assignments for this unit. Your teacher will give you deadlines to work to.

Communicating forensic science: part1

You're a forensic scientist working at the Midshires Forensic Science Laboratory. Due to the increasing public interest in the work of the Forensic Science Service, your centre is planning an open day to display and explain the techniques used in the laboratories.

- Your team has to prepare a handout for the open day to cover its area of expertise.
- The complete set of handouts should cover the major techniques used in the analysis and interpretation of physical and chemical evidence.
- Your teacher will organise your class into teams.
- Each leaflet should be both sides of an A4 sheet.
- Your teacher will give you a topic for your leaflet, taken from:
  - chromatography
  - spectroscopy
  - toxicology
  - marks and impressions
  - trace evidence
  - blood pattern analysis.
- Each member of the team should research the topic. Plan how you will divide up the work. Your handout should include:
  - the methods used
  - how the techniques work
  - what the technique is used for
  - case studies of examples of its uses to solve problems.
- Further guidelines are given below.

topic	include reference to ...
chromatography	TLC, GC and HPLC, uses in toxicology
spectroscopy	UV, IR and mass spectroscopy, uses in toxicology
marks and impressions	footprints and tool marks, recording and methods of comparison
trace evidence	identification and comparison of fibres, glass and paint
blood pattern analysis	blood splatter analysis

- The handout should be written for the *intelligent layperson* (someone who can understand scientific concepts but who has no expert knowledge).

Communicating forensic science: part 2

Your Director decides that anyone should be able to explain any part of work of the centre to anyone who asks about it on the open day.

- One member of a team is to visit another team to receive instruction from that team. Everyone should visit another team at least once. If there are more than four people in your team, pair up for some visits.
- They are to return to their team and pass on the information.
- Open day handouts are to be used to help pass on the information.
- Individuals should keep a record of *key facts* for each topic.

As a team, you will need to decide:

- how many training sessions to hold
- what information to present
- how to use your handout
- who does what
  - in giving training to visitors
  - in receiving training by visiting other teams.

This work may be done during or out of normal class time - but you'll need to fit it in with the practical work sessions.

Organisation

- **Team**: research topic, prepare handout.
- **Individuals**: go to another team to be trained/receive handout. Note time in table.
- **Team**: receive instruction from trained team members. Note agreed time in table.
- **Individuals**: record key facts on each topic.

topic	name of person to receive and pass on training	date/time	team training date/time	tick when done
chromatography				
spectroscopy				
marks and impressions				
trace evidence				
blood pattern analysis				

Key facts

When you've received your training in a topic, record three key facts.

Attach a copy of your handout for your own team's topic.

Topic _____

1 _____

2 _____

3 _____

Topic _____

1 _____

2 _____

3 _____

Topic _____

1 _____

2 _____

3 _____

Topic _____

1 _____

2 _____

3 _____

Fold and attach your handout here.

Topic _____

2: Analytical techniques

The following procedures will give you the opportunity to develop your forensic science practical skills. You will need to work as a forensic scientist to complete the assessed assignments which follow.

Methods of analysis: chromatography

One of the simplest, yet most powerful, methods of analysis is **chromatography**. It makes detailed chemical analysis possible through the physical separation of mixtures.

You are probably already familiar with paper chromatography. Thin layer chromatography (TLC) is similar, but faster and more convenient.

You may work in a group of two or three to carry out the following procedure.

Your task is to separate the dyes in different samples of lipstick, to allow a comparison of their composition. You will:

- be provided with a lipstick sample on a piece of serviette, labelled **1** (such as from a crime scene)

- be given three other pieces of serviette labelled **2**, **3** and **4** (marked with lipstick collected from suspects)

- dissolve the samples in a solvent, prepare the TLC plate and, finally, run the chromatogram.

Standard procedure: Thin layer chromatography of lipstick

Health and safety

A risk assessment must be carried out before starting any procedure. Eluant (3-methylbutan-1-ol, propanone and ammonia solution) [FLAMMABLE, HARMFUL] - work away from naked flames. Wear protective clothing and eye protection.

You will need

centrifuge tubes • centrifuge • wooden splints • scissors • TLC tank or screwtop jar • approximately 5 x 10 cm silica TLC • capillary tubes • hairdryer • eluant (3-methylbutan-1-ol, propanone and ammonia solution) • permanent marker • lipstick samples

Method

Dissolve the samples

1   Label four clean, dry centrifuge tubes 1, 2, 3, 4. Add about 2 cm^3 of eluant to each.

2   Cut out about half of the lipstick sample 1. If serviette is layered, use only the top layer.

3   Use a wooden splint to push the cut-out paper sample to the bottom of tube 1. Mix well by poking and stirring. Leave the splint in the tube.

4   Clean the scissors thoroughly to remove all lipstick.

5   Repeat steps 2-4 for the other three samples of lipstick. Use new wooden splints and appropriately labelled centrifuge tubes.

6   Leave for 10-15 minutes to allow the dyes to dissolve.

7   While waiting, prepare the TLC plate by marking the origins for the samples. Draw a **pencil** line across 1 cm from the bottom (narrower side). Mark four equidistant points and label them 1, 2, 3, 4.

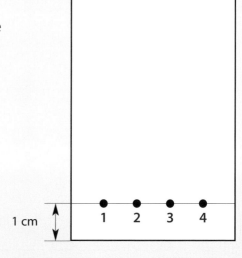

1 cm

Prepare the TLC plate

1   Use the wooden splint in each tube to remove the paper, squeezing it against the side to extract as much solution as possible.

2   Dispose of the paper and splints.

3   Centrifuge the tubes (in pairs or fours so that they balance) for two minutes.

4   Check that you have clear solutions with compacted solid at the bottom. If necessary, centrifuge for another minute.

5   Extract some solution from tube 1 by carefully dipping in a capillary tube. Do not disturb the solid.

6   Transfer one drop on to point 1 on the TLC plate, to make a spot no larger than 3 mm in diameter.

7   Repeat, using clean capillary tubes for the other solutions.

8   Dry with the hair dryer for about 20 seconds and allow to cool for about 10 seconds.

9   Repeat the procedure twice, to add two more drops to each TLC spot. Be careful to keep the spots less than 3 mm in diameter.

Run the chromatogram

1   Pour about a 5 mm depth of eluant into the TLC tank (or jar). It must be less than the height of your spots above the bottom of the plate.

2   Stand the plate in the tank with the origin line at the bottom. Replace the lid and leave for about 30 minutes until the solvent reaches to within about 1 cm from the top.

3   Remove the chromatogram and immediately mark the position of the **solvent front** (the line reached by the eluant), using a **pencil**.

4   Label the plate with an evidence reference number and the date.

Results

Draw scale diagrams (or use scanned images) to show the spots that have separated out for each of the lipstick samples. Make notes to indicate points of similarity or differences.

Do you think any of the samples may have come from the same lipstick?

Explain your answer in a form that could be presented as evidence in court.

You need to explain the evidence and the scientific principle underlying it.

_____

_____

_____

_____

_____

_____

_____

_____

R_f values

When chromatograms are run separately, it's possible to make comparisons using R_f values.

As long as the conditions (type of TLC plate and eluant) are the same, for a given substance R_f is constant:

$$R_f = \frac{\text{distance moved by component}}{\text{distance moved by eluant}} = \frac{\text{distance from baseline to centre of spot}}{\text{distance from baseline to solvent front}}$$

For matching purposes, you don't need to calculate R_f values. All distances are being divided by the same solvent front distance.

However, because R_f values are the same for the same conditions, they can be used to identify components.

Describe an example of when forensic scientists would use chromatography to **identify** substances.

Name:

•   the type of chromatography used

•   the substance(s) involved

•   the reason why the analysis is done.

_____

_____

_____

_____

_____

_____

_____

_____

_____

_____

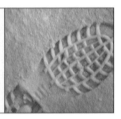

Marks and impressions

Footprints are usually one of the first pieces of evidence to be collected at a crime scene. This is because they are likely to be subject to damage or erosion, especially if outside. Your task is to record crime scene details and make an impression of a footprint.

Technique: Making a cast of a footprint

Health and safety

A risk assessment should be carried out before starting any procedure.

Wear protective clothing and eye protection - casting powder will react with moisture and get hot if it gets in your eyes.

You will need

ruler • camera • cardboard or plastic to make mould • paper clips • casting powder • bottle of water • measuring spoon • disposable plastic bag for mixing • trowel • shoe box or similar • newspaper or other padding • adhesive tape

Method

1   Record the position of the footprint in relation to other parts of the crime scene. Label sketches with your name, a unique reference number and the time and date.

2   Choose the best print to cast and lay a ruler alongside to give scale. Photograph from different angles. (If no camera is available, record by sketching and adding dimensions).

3   Unless the impression is over 1 cm deep, form a dam around it using cardboard or plastic strip fastened with paper clips. Push it part way into the ground without disturbing the footprint.

4   Measure the length and breadth of the cast and estimate the area. Calculate the volume of casting medium needed to give a cast about 1 cm deep.

5   Follow the manufacturer's instructions to mix the correct volume of casting powder and water in the plastic bag. Knead the bag gently to thoroughly mix. You should get a thick and creamy mixture that will pour.

6   Hold the bag by a top and bottom corner and pour half the mixture gently into the print and mould.

7   If available, add a few sticks to reinforce the cast. Pour in the rest of the mixture.

8   When partially set, scratch the reference number and date onto the cast.

9   Allow at least 30 minutes for the cast to set before attempting to move it.

10   Push a trowel or similar tool vertically into the ground alongside the cast and lever it up gently.

11   Retain soil attached to the cast (do not attempt to remove it yet.)

12   Use newspaper or other padding to protect the cast and seal it in a labelled box (reference number, officer's name, date, time, location.)

13   Allow four hours for the cast to fully harden before removing attached soil etc. by gentle brushing or washing.

14   Make labelled sketches to record your observations on the next page.

Footprint cast: distinguishing features

Use labelled diagrams or photographs to record the features you might use to make a match with the original footwear. Record relevant measurements. Use a separate sheet of paper if you need more space.

Trace evidence: burning fibres

Fibres will show a wide range of different characteristics when burned. This makes burning a simple but effective test when trying to identify them. If possible, carry this out in a fume cupboard.

Technique: Fibres burning test

Health and safety

A risk assessment should be carried out before starting any procedure.

You will need

Bunsen burner • heat mat • tongs • crucible • known fibre samples (not necessarily all those in the table of results) • unknown fibre sample

Method

1 Set up the Bunsen burner on a heat proof mat. Light burner and adjust to give a blue flame.

2 Grip one end of a fibre sample in the tongs and ignite the other end in the Bunsen flame.

3 Place the burning sample in crucible. If it goes out, attempt to reignite it as above.

4 Record your observations in the table.

5 Make sure the fibres are fully burnt or extinguished. Clean the crucible before re-using.

6 When all the known samples have been tested, test the unknown and use your observations to attempt to identify it.

fibre	burn rate	burn type	smell	smoke	products
	• slow? • rapid?	• burns easily? • burns on its own?	• hair? • celery? • no smell?	• black? • little? • none?	• crumbly ash? • black ash? • beads? • black beads?
wool					
cotton and linen					
nylon					
acetates					
polyester					
acrylic					
viscose					
unknown					
The unknown fibres are probably:					

Trace evidence: examining fibres

Fibres can be collected and examined using a microscope in the same way as described in the *Biological evidence* section of these worksheets. Refer back to *Microscopic examination of hairs*.

Technique: Microscopic examination of fibres

1   If slides are not to be kept as evidence, make temporary mounts using water instead of DPX or nail varnish.

2   Attempt to confirm your identification of the fibres in the burning test (previous page) by mounting known fibres for comparison with the unknown fibres.

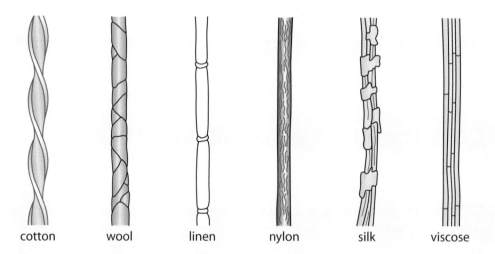

| cotton | wool | linen | nylon | silk | viscose |

3   If possible, use a digital camera to record photomicrographs of your slides.

4   Record your conclusions below.

Results

Can you confirm your burning test identification?

Use descriptions and/or diagrams to support your decision.

Glass density and refractive index

- Different types of glass will have different **densities** and **refractive indices**.
- If two samples of glass have come from the same source, they will have the same densities and refractive indices.

Density

- $$density = \frac{mass}{volume}$$

- The volume of an irregularly shaped piece of broken glass is found by displacing water.

Standard procedure: Finding the density of glass by displacement of water

Health and safety

A risk assessment should be conducted before carrying out any procedure.

Broken glass is very sharp - use forceps to handle.

You will need

balance • 50 and 100 cm^3 measuring cylinders • forceps • pieces of glass

Method

1. Weigh a piece of glass, or several pieces from the same source.
2. Half fill a measuring cylinder, chosen so that the piece of glass will be covered by water. Record the volume as accurately as you can in the table.
3. Place the glass in the measuring cylinder. It must be completely covered by water.
4. Record the *increase* in volume as accurately as you can. (New volume - original volume).
5. Find the density of the glass using:

$$density\ (g/cm^3) = \frac{mass\ /\ g}{increase\ in\ volume\ /\ cm^3}$$

Results

glass sample	volume of water / cm^3	volume of water + glass / cm^3	volume of glass / cm^3	density of glass / g per cm^3
1				
2				
3				
4				
5				

Which glass samples could be from the same source?

_____

Becke lines

- Refractive index describes how much light bends as it passes from one medium to another - for example, from air to glass.

- If a piece of glass is placed into a liquid of the same refractive index, they both have the same effect on the light and the edges will not be visible.

- When refractive indices are different, a dark halo around the edge can be seen with the naked eye. This edge is called the **Becke line**.

- Mounting glass in liquids with different refractive indices can be used to estimate the refractive index of very small glass samples.

Standard procedure: Finding the refractive index of glass using Becke lines

Health and safety

A risk assessment should be conducted before carrying out any procedure.

You will need

clean microscope slides • forceps • small glass fragments •
range of oils with different refractive indices • wax pencil or fine permanent marker pen

Method

1   Label slides with the refractive index (RI) of each oil to be used.

2   Use forceps to place a glass fragment on a slide.

3   Add a drop of the oil with the RI, as on the label.

4   View with a microscope, starting with the lowest power to locate the glass fragment.

5   Choose the power that's easiest to use to see the Becke line (a dark halo at the edge of the glass).

   - **If the line is inside the glass, the liquid has a lower RI than the glass.**

   - **If the line is outside the glass, the liquid has a higher RI than the glass.**

6   Choose an oil with a RI that is likely to be closer to the glass and find the Becke line again for a new glass fragment and slide.

7   Continue until there is no Becke line or the RI of the glass lies between the RIs of two oils.

8   Record the values below.

Results

Refractive index of glass is _____

(record actual value if no Becke line or *between ... and ...*)

Paint fragments

Paint fragments are seldom a single colour or a single layer.

This makes them useful for forming links between suspects and crime scenes or victims - if colours and their sequence can be matched, it's not likely to be simple coincidence.

Your task is to use light microscopy to compare the layers in paint samples.

Standard procedure: Microscopic examination of paint fragments

Health and safety

A risk assessment should be conducted before carrying out any procedure. Use PAT tested microscopes and lamps.

You will need

microscope • lamp • microscope slides • black paper • *Blu-Tack* •
paint fragments in separate labelled samples • forceps • fine permanent marker

Method

1   Flatten a small piece of *Blu-Tack* onto the centre of a microscope slide.

2   Label the slide with the reference number or name of the sample to be investigated.

3   Use forceps to fix a paint sample vertically on edge in the *Blu-Tack*.

4   Place the microscope slide on the microscope stage. Line up the sample with the objective lens.

5   Switch on the illumination of the microscope and use the low power to locate the sample. Do not attempt to focus accurately at this stage.

6   Switch off any under stage illumination and use a lamp to illuminate the sample from above.

7   Focus and move the sample, refocusing as necessary, until distinct layers can be seen.

8   Experiment with using other powers. When you have the best image that you can, sketch a labelled diagram in the results table below.

9   If you can, record a digital image of the paint layers and attach to this page.

10   Repeat the procedure for at least two more paint samples.

Results

Appearance of edge of paint samples:

sample reference:	sample reference:

sample reference:	sample reference:

Questions

1   Which samples might be from the same source? Explain your decision.

_____

_____

_____

_____

_____

_____

2   Which samples do not match? Explain.

_____

_____

_____

_____

_____

_____

Blood splatter analysis

Your task is to investigate the effect of height and angle of impact on blood splatter patterns.

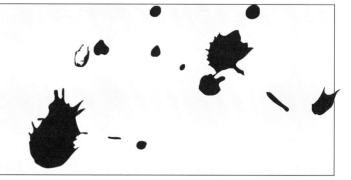

Vertical drip blood patterns

Health and safety

A risk assessment should be made before carrying out any procedure.

You will need

artificial blood · teat pipette · metre rule or measuring tape · 15 cm ruler with mm scale ·
A4 plain paper · graph paper · 5 cm^3 measuring cylinder

Method: single blood drips

Record your observations in the results table.

1. Place a sheet of plain A4 paper on the floor.

2. Use the teat pipette to drip one drop of artificial blood on to the paper from a height of 10 cm.

3. Move the pipette to get two more separate patterns on the paper.

4. Label the blood spots as 10 cm.

5. Repeat to get three more blood spots for each of these heights: 20, 40, 60, 80, 100, 120 and 150 cm. Space the spots so they don't overlap. Use a new sheet of paper if you need to.

6. Allow the blood spots to dry. Measure the diameter of the circular part of each to the nearest millmetre. When measuring, ignore any protrusions (bits of the spot that stick out from the central circular part).

7. Sketch the actual shape of each spot, showing the direction of any protrusions.

Method: multiple blood drips

Record your observations in the results table.

1. Using the same technique as above, drip one drop of artificial blood onto a sheet of plain A4 paper from a height of 30 cm.

2. Keeping the pipette at the same height, drip another drop onto the first one.

3. Repeat for two more drops.

4. Use a clean sheet of target paper.

5. Measure 2 cm^3 of artificial blood into a 5 cm^3 measuring cylinder.

6. Pour all the blood onto the target paper from a height of 30 cm.

Results table

single vertical blood drips		
height of blood drip / cm	diameter of blood spots / mm	sketch of blood spots
10	 mean =	
20	 mean =	
40	 mean =	
60	 mean =	
80	 mean =	
100	 mean =	
120	 mean =	
150	 mean =	

multiple vertical blood drips	
number of blood drips	observations, description and drawing
one	
two	
three	
four	
large volume (2 cm^3)	

Method: different surfaces

If time permits, you may wish to try the effect obtained when single blood drops are dripped on to different surfaces (e.g. tiles, cardboard, newspaper, plastic) from a height of 30 cm. Ask your teacher.

Questions

1 How are the blood spots from different heights alike?

_____

_____

2 How do blood spots from different heights differ?

_____

_____

3 How do the large volume and dripped blood patterns contrast?

_____

_____

4 Circular blood spots with the following diameters were found at the scene of a crime. What approximate height did they fall from?

10 mm _____

15 mm _____

20 mm _____

Blood dripping at an angle

Health and safety
A risk assessment should be conducted before carrying out any procedure.

You will need
clipboard • adhesive tape • protractor • artificial blood • teat pipette • metre rule or measuring tape • 15 cm ruler with mm scale • A4 plain paper • graph paper • 5 cm^3 measuring cylinder

Method

1 Tape the lower end of the clipboard to the bench top, to act as a hinge.

2 Clip a sheet of plain A4 paper to the clipboard.

3 Write **Impact angle 10°** on the paper.

4 Using the protractor, raise the clipboard to an angle of 80° to the bench surface. This will give an impact angle of (90-80)° = 10° when the blood is dripped vertically.

5 Use the teat pipette to drip one drop of artificial blood onto the paper from a height of 30 cm.

6 Keeping the same height, move the pipette to get two more blood drop patterns on the paper.

7 Record your observations in the results table.

8 Repeat for the remaining impact angles in the table.

Results table

impact angle / °	mean length of spot / mm	mean width of spot / mm	sketch	description
10				
30				
50				
70				
90				

• Plot a graph of *width* or *length of blood spot* against *angle of impact*.

Questions

1   In which direction does the *tail* on the blood spot point in relation to where it came from?

_____

_____

_____

_____

2   How do the following change as impact angle increases?

length of blood spot:

_____

_____

width of blood spot:

_____

_____

3   Explain why the analysis of blood splatter patterns is useful to the forensic investigator.

_____

_____

_____

_____

_____

_____

_____

1: More fantastic than *Taggart*: A case study

Even the defence attorney described this case as more fantastic than an episode of *Taggart*:

> *"If someone had gone along to the producers of Taggart and said, 'I have a script that involves a church, a girl from Poland, a priest, a handyman, all the cast of characters led in this case', don't you think it is at least a possibility they would say, 'Go away and come back with something people will believe, because they will not believe that'?"*

Yet the events described in this case study are true. The crime took place in Glasgow. Although Scotland has its own criminal justice system, it shares many similarities with the rest of the UK. The case demonstrates the scope of the work done by SOCOs and forensic scientists at the scene of the crime, in the laboratory and in court.

The key *characters* included ...

- Angelika Kluk, 23, the victim. She was a Polish student who came to Scotland to earn money from holiday work to support her studies. Her gagged and bound body was found under the floor of St Patrick's Church in Glasgow.

- Peter Tobin, 60, the accused. A handyman known as Pat McLaughlin, he worked at the church where Angelika had a room.

- Aneta Kluk, 28, sister of the murdered girl.

- Detective Superintendent David Swindle, who led the police enquiry.

- Father Gerry Nugent, 63, who gave Angelika a room at the church. He had an open door policy for the homeless.

- Martin Macaskill, 40, married chauffeur who was having an affair with Angelika, with his wife's knowledge.

- Annie Macaskill, wife of Martin. She tried to accept her husband's relationship with Angelika while maintaining her marriage.

- Sheriff Kieran McLernan, 65, who befriended Angelika and was with her the night before she died.

- Julie McAdam, a consultant pathologist.

- Carol Weston, 33, a forensic scientist who went to the crime scene and gave detailed evidence in court.

- Martin Fairley, 45, a forensic scientist who analysed DNA and gave detailed evidence in court.

- David Thurley, a crime scene expert.

- Catherine Boyle, a fingerprint expert.

- Matthew Spark-Egan, 37, who heard the sounds of something being dragged while he was in the church.

- Marie Devine, 64, a parishioner at St Patrick's Church who saw Tobin and Angelika having a cup of tea together on the day she disappeared.

- PC David Dick, 46, a dog handler who searched for Angelika.

- Sergeant Steven McPhelim, who found the body.

- PC Alan Murray who arrested Tobin at a London hospital where he had aroused suspicion. He dressed as a nurse to identify Tobin.

- Donald Finlay, Tobin's defence lawyer.

- Dorothy Bain, the prosecuting lawyer.

- Lord Menzies, the judge.

Read the case study and answer the questions on a separate sheet of paper.

When arrested, Tobin was accused of attacking Angelika between 24 and 29 September in St Patrick's Church, or elsewhere, gagging her with cloth and tape, binding her hands with cable ties, raping her, smashing her skull with a piece of wood or something similar, stabbing her 16 times in the chest and inflicting other knife injuries.

Part of the defence's case was based on the possibility that witnesses might themselves have been involved in the murder.

* **Which of the *characters* in the case are themselves potentially guilty of the murder?**

* **In this case, how might forensic evidence help to convict the guilty but clear the innocent?**

When Angelica was reported missing, a search was made of the church and grounds. A police dog, Delta, was used but found nothing.

* **Why was a dog used?**

* **Suggest a possible reason why the dog did not find Angelika.**

The day before Angelika's body was discovered, her room had been searched and a forensic photographer had recorded evidence, which included her diary.

In this she had recorded her first meeting with Martin Macaskill. She wrote:

"Martin is a very nice man. It is a pity most nice men are already taken. He is not too old either, merely 40."

A message signed *Martin* was also found in a book. It read:

"To Angela. I will always carry your song in my heart. You are my aghrai [darling]. I will always love you."

* **Why was Angelika's room searched before her body was found?**

* **Why was a photographer used to record evidence?**

During the trial, Sergeant Steven McPhelim, took the stand to explain what the search team found. A reconnaissance of the church and grounds led them to a small hatch, covered by carpet. He described to the court what he saw as a colleague opened the hatch.

"It was quite dark but I could see what appeared to be a blue coloured tarpaulin or plastic sheeting. I then moved my position slightly and I could see what appeared to be two arms sticking out under the tarpaulin."

* **What do you think was the main method used to record both what Sergeant McPhelim saw and the subsequent recovery of Angelika's body?**

Martin Fairley carried out DNA analysis of evidence from the crime scene. In court, he was said to have 24-years experience.

* **Why was this significant?**

Martin Fairley, told the court he had found DNA matching Mr Tobin on a gag that had been wound tightly round Angelika's head. Dorothy Bain, prosecuting, asked if it was a reasonable conclusion to make that he (Mr Tobin) touched the tape. Martin Fairley replied:

"I think it is a reasonable conclusion."

Carol Weston gave further evidence by describing the painstaking process of collecting evidence from the crime scene. She told how the bound and blood-stained body could be seen through a small hatch near the priest's confessional. No blood-stains were found on the floor or the hatch but a search for DNA was undertaken. Swabs were also taken from the student's body. She said:

"I was under the floor about, I think, for just under three hours."

She said that a fingerprint on the tape provided DNA which closely matched the accused, Peter Tobin, but said in hindsight she should have swabbed the whole tape.

* **How can forensic scientists get enough DNA for DNA profiling from a fingerprint?**

* **Why should she have swabbed the whole tape?**

Father Gerry Nugent, 63, gave a DNA sample to detectives investigating the student's murder. But forensic scientist Carol Weston said the test had shown nothing to link the priest to Angelika's death. She told the court that Father Nugent, and a number of other people, had been asked to give DNA samples for elimination purposes. They included Angelika's married lover, Martin Macaskill, and his wife Anne. She said there was no evidence to link any of them, in terms of DNA profiles, to Angelika's dead body.

•   **Does this prove that these people were not involved in the murder?**

Carol Weston also described how a fleece jacket and a tarpaulin sheet with Angelika's blood on them had been found. She said the blood smears would be consistent with a body being wrapped in a sheet and then slid under the church floor. Computer generated graphics were shown to the jury, to illustrate how Angelika's body could have been dropped down below the church floor. However, no trace of blood could be found along the likely route between the garage, where the attack was thought to take place, and the hole in the floor.

•   **How would the forensic scientists have searched for blood?**

•   **How would forensic scientists confirm that the stains were blood?**

•   **Do you think that computer graphics were useful here? Explain your answer.**

Tobin's prints were found on items dumped with Angelika's body. Fingerprint expert Catherine Boyle said the impressions from fingers and palms were found on plastic sheeting and on a black plastic bag.

•   **Does this confirm that Tobin dumped the body?**

Julie McAdam, a pathologist, examined the body and gave evidence about the cause and time of death. When questioned by the prosecutor, Dorothy Bain, Dr McAdam said the cause of death was stab wounds to the chest, head injuries and occlusion of the mouth by gagging. She told the court that Angelika was hit over the head six times and stabbed 16 times in the chest. She said that she had been hit with something heavy, fracturing her skull. Detectives were sent to look for something with angles after the pathologist had examined the head wounds.

Later, the jury was also told that a blood-stained table leg was found at the church, propped up against an outside wall. Crime scene expert David Thurley said four table legs were found around the outside of the church. He said that small pieces of protruding wood on the legs matched a piece found in the blood-stained and paint-splattered plastic sheet which was under the church floor with Angelika's body. One of the table legs, bearing traces of paint, was shown to the court.

The chair leg which may have been used as a weapon to attack Angelika contained no DNA from Tobin. Under cross examination from Donald Findlay, defending Mr Tobin, forensic scientist Carol Weston said:

"I don't believe we found Mr Tobin's DNA on the knife. We only found Angelika Kluk's DNA on the table leg."

•   **What would the forensic scientists have done to try and match the pieces of wood?**

•   **How might the traces of paint have been significant?**

•   **Before the pathologist began to give evidence, members of the public were asked to leave the court to allow photographs to be shown. Suggest a reason why members of the public were asked to leave.**

Dr McAdam said she had tried to work out from the injuries what had happened - beginning with blows to the back and side of Angelika's head. A finger was broken and hands bruised as she instinctively put them up to her head.

"If she were not unconscious she would have been stunned," the consultant pathologist said. *"Possibly this would have given her assailant time to bind her and gag her without too much of a struggle."*

Despite being gagged and bound, Dr McAdam, 35, said she thought Angelika tried to fight back. Her attempt to shield her body led to the blade piercing right through her left wrist.

•   **Suggest some reasons why it is important for details of a violent crime to be reported in court.**

Dr McAdam also stated that:

"The fact that there was no rigor, this means she had definitely been dead over 36 hours. However, given the condition she was in, and given other findings of decomposition, I would estimate she had been dead for at least several days."

- She said that her findings were in keeping with Angelika being dead six days earlier, on Sunday 24 September at about 1800 BST. Why was this important evidence?
- What evidence might the defence have used to suggest that there was enough reasonable doubt to <u>not</u> convict Tobin?

The forensic evidence was enough for the jury to take only three and a half hours to convict Peter Tobin. He was sentenced to life imprisonment with a minimum term of 21 years.

Lord Menzies said:

"The attack on Angelika Kluk was inhuman. You are, in my view, an evil man," adding that Tobin had showed *"contempt and disdain for the life of a young woman with her whole life ahead of her".*

Ms Kluk's sister Aneta, 28, sitting in the public gallery, shouted thank you to the jury after their unanimous verdict was announced. In a statement she said she and her father were grateful that her sister's killer was likely to spend the rest of his days behind bars.

Postscript

Peter Tobin is to be interviewed by murder detectives about the unsolved case of Vicky Hamilton, who was last seen alive in 1991. The case was reopened as a murder investigation and detectives began poring over the 7000 interviews, 4000 statements and 12 000 documents from one of Scotland's biggest ever missing person inquiries. They hope advances in DNA techniques will provide a vital clue to the identity of her killer. A black leather purse found close to Edinburgh's St Andrew Square bus station 11 days after she went missing has also been undergoing fresh analysis.

Assessment overview

Completing the worksheet section will have helped you develop knowledge, understanding and skills employed by Scene of Crime Officers and Forensic Scientists.

You will need to demonstrate these skills to successfully complete the first three assignments: *Investigating a crime scene*, *Analysing evidence* and *Acting as an expert witness*.

Acting as an expert witness also requires you to write and present a clear report of your work and findings.

For the fourth assignment, *Forensic science services*, you will use your understanding of forensic procedures and will need to carry out some further research on the criminal justice system.

*   *Investigating a crime scene* and *Analysing evidence* are based on the collection and analysis of valid evidence from a crime scene.

*   *Acting as an expert witness* is a written report of your actions and findings, to be presented in court.

*   *Forensic science services* is based on teamwork to collect and share information. You then produce an individual report of the role of the forensic science service within the criminal justice system.

You will be given further guidance by your teacher, including assignment frontsheets on which you should write your deadlines. Be careful to plan your work so you can meet them comfortably.

Remember: you may need to revisit some work if you don't achieve the criteria the first time. Your teacher will give you further guidance, as necessary.

Be sure to ask whenever you are unsure about something.

You will be expected to:

*   work independently

*   work safely with regard to yourself and others

*   competently follow laboratory procedures.

ASSIGNMENT - INVESTIGATING A CRIME SCENE

Scenario

A crime has been committed. As a Scene of Crime Officer, you will be briefed by the first responder about the crime scene. Further evidence may come to light if suspects are identified. You will be required to:

- safely record and preserve valid evidence from the scene
- explain how valid evidence has been obtained
- determine how the valid evidence collected could be used in a criminal investigation.

Task 1

Acting on advice from the first responder, you must conduct an intial search, record the scene and target two types of biological and two types of physical and chemical evidence.

For each of the four types of evidence, use techniques and procedures *as appropriate* to conduct a search, record and document, collect and recover (preventing contamination) and package and label.

If you complete task 1 correctly you will meet grading criterion P1

Task 2

Write a short report to decribe the techniques that you used to process the crime scene and to explain how they enabled you to obtain valid forensic evidence.

If you complete task 2 correctly you will meet grading criterion M1

Task 3

Write a short report to evaluate the processing of the crime scene by suggesting how the valid evidence collected could be used in a criminal investigation.

If you complete task 3 correctly you will meet grading criterion D1

Guidelines

P1 **Efficient** refers to correctly collecting the useful targeted evidence within a reasonable time scale.

Effective means *fit for purpose*. Here it refers to working safely, using techniques correctly and maintaining the usefulness and validity of the evidence.

Valid means the evidence is true and maintains its legal force.

You will be observed carrying out the collection of the evidence and will need a witness statement for your portfolio. Make sure you choose and use effective search techniques, prevent contamination of the scene and evidence, and record and label evidence correctly so that the chain of continuity can be maintained.

M1 Your report will need to describe how what you did contributed to the validity of the evidence.

D1 You will need to reflect on the advantages and limitations of the evidence and how it might be used in identifying suspects and convicting a criminal.

ASSIGNMENT - ANALYSING EVIDENCE

Scenario

As a forensic scientist, you will receive evidence from a crime scene. Further evidence may be collected from suspects. You will need to:

- plan and safely carry out the analysis of biological, physical and chemical evidence and data
- draw conclusions, describing and explaining patterns and connections in your results
- suggest improvements in the techniques and procedures you used.

Task 1

Acting as the forensic scientist who receives the evidence from the crime scene for laboratory analysis, you should state your objectives and write and carry out a plan to effectively analyse the two types of biological evidence obtained.

If you complete task 1 correctly you will meet grading criterion P2

Task 2

Write a short report to draw conclusions for your investigation of biological evidence and describe how well the outcomes of your investigation met your objectives.

If you complete task 2 correctly you will meet grading criterion M2

Task 3

Write and justify the choice of suggestions for improvements to the plans to investigate biological evidence.

If you complete task 3 correctly you will meet grading criterion D2

Task 4

Acting as the forensic scientist who receives the evidence from the crime scene for laboratory analysis, you should write a plan to effectively analyse data from the the two types of physical and chemical evidence obtained.

If you complete task 4 correctly you will meet grading criterion P3

Task 5

Write a short report to:

(a) describe patterns and make relevant connections in the data for physical and chemical evidence
(b) explain the patterns found and make relevant connections.

If you complete task 5 (a) correctly you will meet grading criterion M3

If you complete task 5 (b) correctly you will meet grading criterion D3

Guidelines

P2 and P3

Plan means that you need to describe what you are going to do and also what you will need to do it. You should

- state the objectives that your plan is designed to meet
- list the techniques and procedures that you are going to use
- produce a request list for the materials and equipment that you need.

M2 Conclusions describe what your results show. Did your investigation do what you hoped it would to give you what you needed to meet your objectives?

D2 **Justify** means that you need to describe and explain what you would need to do to get more useful conclusions. Is anything missing or could stronger evidence be obtained?

M3 What conclusions can you form concerning the patterns in the data? What relationships are shown? What kinds of changes take place? What things are linked together? What links can you make between the data and the crime?

D3 What is the significance of the patterns? What has caused the patterns and connections? Why have they occurred?

You should:

- target evidence to demonstrate that you can recognise the significance of evidence
- choose and use techniques to show that you understand why and how the correct techniques must be used
- as necessary:
    - anticipate problems and implement contingency plans
    - modify procedures and techniques to overcome problems
- suggest changes to procedures to enable better evidence to be obtained
- match the outcomes to the objectives of your investigation
- describe and analyse patterns in your data
- evaluate quantitative and qualitative data
- draw conclusions and interpret them
- explain the meaning of the evidence and recognise the relevance of your conclusions to the crime investigation.

ASSIGNMENT – ACTING AS AN EXPERT WITNESS

Scenario

As the scientist who has collected and analysed the evidence from a crime scene, you will be required to act as an expert witness. You will need to prepare a statement to give evidence in court.

Task

As a Scene of Crime Officer or forensic scientist, you will be expected to act as an expert witness. For one investigation, prepare a written statement to give evidence in court which:

(a1) • identifies each technique used to obtain evidence

• describes the conclusions of the investigation

(b1) • describes the techniques used to obtain evidence

• explains the conclusions

(c1) • evaluates the techniques used to obtain evidence

• justifies the conclusions

Choose an investigation which you think gives clear evidence that might be used to prosecute or defend an accused person.

Courtroom role play

Members of your class will act as:

• **Judge** • **Prosecuting lawyer** • **Defence lawyer** • **Jury**

Your statement may be used as evidence for the prosecution or for the defence. Decide this in advance.

Procedure

1 Present your statement to the judge and jury.

2 Lawyers acting for the prosecution and defence take turns to question your evidence.

3 The judge advises the jury on what they consider to be the legal validity of the evidence.

4 The jury discusses the evidence and considers how it supports either the prosecution or the defence.

The jury should consider whether:

(a2) • techniques were identified appropriately

• valid conclusions were formed

(b2) • techniques were described accurately

• conclusions were explained adequately

(c2) • use of the techniques was assessed fully

• reasons for the conclusions were suitably justified.

The considerations of the jury will be used to help decide which grading criteria have been met.

If you complete task (a1 and a2) correctly you will meet grading criterion P4

If you complete task (b1 and b2) correctly you will meet grading criterion M4

If you complete task (c1 and c2) correctly you will meet grading criterion D4

Guidelines

P4 The statement should be clear to any person who might appear on the jury, so technical terms should be explained when necessary.

M4 Descriptions of the techniques should pay special attention to any controls or precautions used to ensure the validity of the evidence.

D4 Describe and explain the strengths and weaknesses of the techniques used. Show the extent to which the evidence supports the conclusions.

You should:

- write your report in a concise format that will allow it to be read out in court
- use terminology correctly
- describe patterns and state conclusions clearly
- explain how the conclusions are based on the evidence.

ASSIGNMENT - FORENSIC SCIENCE SERVICE

Scenario

You're a new recruit to the Midshires Regional Forensic Science Laboratory. As a good communicator with an up-to-date knowledge of the system, you've been asked to prepare a leaflet - *The Forensic Science Service and the Criminal Justice System* - for the general public.

- Work in a group of four or five to do background research and exchange ideas.
- Prepare and construct your own leaflet. It's important that this is your own work.
- Use a single A4 sheet, which can be printed on both sides. It may be folded in half or into thirds.

Task 1

Use headings and lists to summarise the components of the criminal justice system and the tasks undertaken by the forensic science service.

If you complete task 1 correctly you will meet grading criterion P5

Task 2

Use case studies to show how members of the forensic science service interact with the other parts of the criminal justice system.

If you complete task 2 correctly you will meet grading criterion M5

Task 3

Using examples from case studies, give the reasons why members of the forensic science service interact with other parts of the criminal justice system. This may be in addition to or integrated with Task 2.

If you complete task 3 correctly you will meet grading criterion D5

Guidelines

P5 Use lists and headings only, to summarise the different parts of the criminal justice system and the jobs done by the forensic science service that relate to this.

M5 Show how criminal investigations, the law and the criminal justice system are linked to forensic science.

D5 Use examples to explain how the forensic science service helps criminal investigations to achieve justice through the law and the criminal justice system.

You will need to show how the forensic science service fits into and supports the whole system that is designed to protect and sustain our society by ensuring justice and upholding the law.

ESSENTIAL KNOWLEDGE AND DATA

What does it mean?

The word *forensic* comes from *forum*. It relates to presenting evidence in a court of law. Forensic science is the application of scientific procedures to uphold the law.

Forensic fiction

You might have read books or watched films or TV programmes with forensic scientists at work. It's all drama and excitement, with grisly crimes and unforeseen conclusions. Amazing deductions are made from tiny pieces of evidence, often by brilliant scientists working alone.

Real life is different!

- Forensic scientists work in teams, drawing on a wide range of expertise. Scene of Crime Officers (SOCOs) and laboratory investigators all have their special tasks to do, depending on the evidence at the scene of the crime.

- The work has to be precise and painstaking. Nothing must be overlooked. Everything must be recorded carefully so there can be no doubt that evidence is true and accurate.

- Sometimes evidence is needed to show that *no* crime has been committe, for example, in an accident or natural disaster. Defence teams use forensic evidence as well as prosecutors.

- Forensic scientists must work safely to protect themselves and others from harm. They must be able to identify hazards and risks and take safety precautions.

SOCOs

SOCOs use special search and collection techniques. For example:

- They search for fibres and hairs with different light sources, such as portable UV lamps. The fibre/hairs can be collected using forceps or sticky tape.

- They vacuum carpets and furniture using new bags to pick up trace materials missed by the investigators.

- They search for fingerprints with different light sources, or make them more visible using dusts. Fingerprints are photographed before being lifted or transferred onto a material that can be taken to the lab.

- They photograph and make casts of tool or tyre marks, footprints and bite marks.

- They collect samples of blood and other body fluids using swabs. Blood stain patterns are photographed and sketched.

Teamwork

Members of a team usually specialise in one area of science, such as chemistry, medicine, pathology, physics, psychology, biology or photography. They then train to get forensic science qualifications.

Most teams include sub-units such as biology, photography, firearms, documents and fingerprints. Smaller teams send evidence to specialists for expert analysis. Even big departments call on specialist help if needed.

Specialist help incudes experts such as pathologists (who specialise in identifing causes of death) and odontologists (who are experts in identifying remains using teeth). They often use specialist equipment in university research labs.

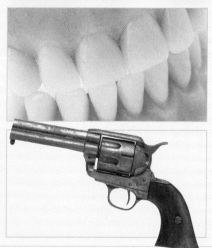

Forensic scientists working in labs analyse evidence. For example they ...

- match hairs and fibres or glass and paint fragments
- determine blood groups and DNA profiles
- match fingerprints to databases
- match bullets to guns using characteristic marks
- determine cause of death from tissue damage or tests for drugs and poisons
- estimate time of death from insects or condition of body tissues
- test for fire accelerants in suspected arson cases.

Safe working

According to COSHH regulations (Control of Substances Hazardous to Health), employers must control exposure to hazardous substances to prevent ill health.

By law, your employers are responsible for providing you with safe working conditions.

But ultimately it's up to you to make decisions and inform them if hazards cause unacceptable risks.

After your employer has done their part, you are responsible for your own safety and the safety of others you might affect.

Hazard or risk?

According to the Health and Safety Executive, *Five steps to risk assessment ...*

'A hazard is anything that may cause harm, such as chemicals, electricity, working from ladders, an open drawer etc.'

The risk is the chance, high or low, that somebody could be harmed by these and other hazards, together with an indication of how serious the harm could be.'

So, it's possible to carry out a risk assessment and take action to reduce the risk associated with any hazard. Such action could include the use of personal protective equipment (PPE) and the safe disposal of wastes.

The *five steps to risk assessment* are

1 Identify the hazards.

2 Decide who might be harmed and how.

3 Evaluate the risks and decide on precautions.

4 Record your findings and implement them.

5 Review your assessment and update if necessary.

Some examples of COSHH warning labels ...

TOXIC

CORROSIVE

EXPLOSIVE

OXIDISING

HARMFUL

FLAMMABLE

Hazards at a crime scene or in the lab

Scientists encounter different hazards in the field and in the laboratory depending on the work they do.

For example, SOCOs might have to attend the scene of a traffic accident, terrorist bombing or a field recently sprayed with chemicals.

They need to assess the hazards and take action to reduce the risks to acceptable levels. This often involves the use of personal protective equipment (PPE) such as gloves or face masks.

Chemicals

The Chemicals (Hazard Information and Packaging for Supply) Regulations 2002 is known as CHIP3. It requires suppliers of dangerous chemicals to package chemicals safely and give safety information on the package and in safety data sheets (SDS).

For most chemicals, a label will indicate if COSHH applies, for example:

• household washing up liquid - no warning label - can be used at work without a risk assessment

• bleach - has a warning label - at work, a risk assessment must be carried out before use.

Sharps

Sharp instruments and objects like scalpel blades or glass fragments require special attention. Not only can they cause injury, but wounds may allow harmful substances such as poisons or disease-causing organisms to enter the body. For example, hypodermic needles contaminated with blood can transmit hepatitis or HIV.

Employers are required to give training on safe working practice, including safe handling and disposal. A sharps disposal kit might include disposable gloves, tongs and a puncture resistant sharps container. Biologically contaminated sharps need special, clearly labelled clinical waste containers.

Scene of crime officers (SOCOs):

- collect evidence
- act as expert witnesses in courts of law.

They must use the correct techniques to effectively search crime scenes and recover valid evidence.

Valid Evidence

Valid evidence is based on the **truth**. It can be accepted in court. You can use two procedures to make sure evidence is valid:

- avoid contamination
- record accurately.

Great care is needed in both cases. For example, a SOCO could leave their own fingerprints or hairs on evidence.

Russell Bradbury was convicted of rape nearly twenty years after he committed the crime. Scientists used a carefully stored and documented microcope slide to obtain his DNA profile. It's an example of how correctly collected, stored and documented evidence can be used years later.

Scene of crime officers wear protective clothing to avoid contamination. Overalls, hoods, masks, surgical gloves and shoe protectors prevent fibres, hairs and fluids from investigators from mixing with evidence at the scene.

Action at the scene of the crime

The first person at the scene of an incident is the **first responder**. It's often a police officer, but it could be anyone, including you. You would need to think fast to ensure safety and preserve evidence.

As a first responder, you should	Notes
ensure safety	You first - you can't do anything if you are injured.
give emergency first aid	Try to avoid washing casualties or removing clothing, you may remove evidence.
detain and remove any suspect	This needs a police officer.
secure the crime scene to prevent contamination	Mark off the area to keep people away (you can use ropes, flags or special tape).
record and preserve evidence that may be destroyed or lost	Some evidence is fragile, for example it might be blown or washed away by the wind or rain.
locate and separate witnesses	If witnesses talk to each other, their testimony may not hold up in court.
make field notes and sketches	Record your observations, so that when the scene of crime team arrives you can give them information rapidly.

The exchange principle

Whenever you make contact with another person, place or object, physical materials like hairs or fibres are exchanged. These physical materials are **trace evidence**. Investigators search for trace evidence from the suspect, the scene and the victim. Matching samples can link the suspect to the scene and victim.

What exchanges have you made today? Have a quick look at your clothes and shoes. Are there any foreign hairs, fibres or stains? What's sticking to the soles of your shoes? Have you stolen a doughnut or smoked an illicit cigarette? How could a forensic scientist tell?

Searching for evidence

Searching has to be thorough and right first time. If not, it might change or destroy the evidence. There are three main steps in retrieving evidence:

1 Initial assessment

Using information from the first responder, you walk through the scene making notes and sketches. You are trying to build up the *big picture*. Include:

- safety issues
- deciding where to cordon off scene boundaries
- need to protect evidence
- whereabouts of visible evidence
- suggestions on likely evidence
- positions of entry and exit points
- need for special resources.

Concentrate on where the crime was committed (or body if present) and the entrances and exits to the scene. You do not normally collect any evidence at this stage.

Searching for evidence (cont ...)

2 Systematic search

After the initial assessment a search is planned and carried out. Just how depends on the number of investigators and the time they have.

3 Targeting

Targeting saves time and resources. The search should match the crime, e.g. looking for

- paint, glass and plastic fragments for a road accident

- blood, hairs, fibres and body fluids for an assault.

Search routines are chosen from:

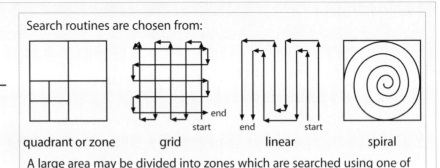

quadrant or zone   grid   linear   spiral

A large area may be divided into zones which are searched using one of the other routines. The grid method allows the area to be covered twice. Searching may be divided between members of a team, e.g. investigators may line up to cross from one side of a field to another (linear pattern) then repeat at right angles (completes grid). A spiral can start from the centre or from the outside.

Investigators still keep an eye open for other evidence. Samples of materials that might have been transferred to a suspect are taken. These are called **reference samples**. They might include things like soil, carpet fibres, glass or paint fragments that were there before the incident.

Documentation and recovery of evidence

Photography is an excellent way to record evidence. You can take photographs without moving or disturbing anything at the scene. You can put numbered cards in key places so they appear in the photos. Your notes can refer to them, e.g. *glass fragments were found at position 3*. If you use a video camera, you can record yourself or others describing the scene.

A detailed **sketch map** can be used to record evidence. Adding measurements gives the precise positions.

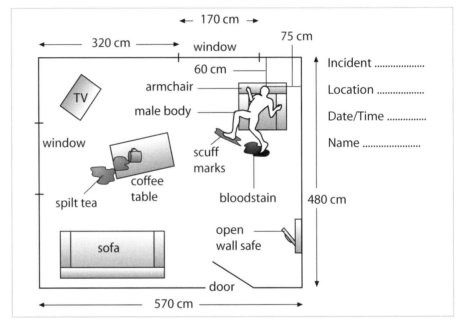

Collect, bag and label

Careful **collection, bagging and labelling** of evidence reduces the possibility of **contamination**. Traces like fibres must not be mixed with each other, or other traces from the crime scene or investigators. Evidence must be put into suitable, clean containers.

- Small, dry materials can be folded in clean paper and placed in envelopes, plastic bags or paper bags sealed with tape.

- Sharp items, like glass fragments, are folded in paper and put into tubes, such as film cans.

- Larger items can be wrapped in paper, taped and placed in strong cardboard boxes.

- Wet samples can be put into airtight containers, such as metal boxes or glass tubes. For storage, they are air dried, frozen or refrigerated to prevent decay.

All evidence is labelled with:

- case number

- name of officer who found it

- date and time

- notes describing the object (its condition, where it was found).

Careful documenting continues to maintain a **chain of continuity** from crime scene to court.

Any person handling the evidence or removing it for testing signs and dates it, including time and purpose.

This continuous monitoring is essential all the way to the court, as proof that the evidence has not been tampered with.

Biological trace evidence

Criminals often leave biological traces at the scene of a crime. Examples include:

- hair
- fingerprints
- blood and other body fluids.

DNA may often be extracted from such material. Teeth, bones and other remains of victims can also provide clues, as can insects attracted to decaying bodies.

We shed about 100 hairs every day. They are often lost if there is a violent struggle. They can be found at the scene of 70% of crimes in which the victim dies.

Evidence from hairs

The microscopic structure of human hairs can vary in many ways. Hair from different animal species can be identified. So, it's possible to match hairs you find on a victim or at the crime scene to hairs found on a suspect or at their home.

If the hair root is attached, **DNA profiling** is possible. This will give an almost unique match (see section on *DNA profiling*). Hairs can also contain detectable traces of drugs and poisons (see sections on *Methods of analysis* and *Toxicology*). As hair grows at a fairly constant rate, it's possible to estimate the time at which the hair was exposed to dye, perm or other chemicals, including drugs in the blood.

Hair structure

Hairs have three basic parts: the **cuticle**, **cortex** and **medulla**. The medulla in most human hair is absent or fragmented. Larger ovoid bodies are common in some animals, but vary greatly in human hair. Air spaces of varying sizes and shapes can also be present.

- **Colour**

  Pigment granules vary according to the colour of the hair; human hair may be dyed.

- **Shape**

  Straight, wavy or curly.

- **Thickness**

  Hair from the same person and part of the body is of similar thickness; animal hair tends to be thinner than human hair.

- **Surface (cuticle)**

  Each animal species has characteristic scales; human scales are flat and hard to see.

- **Ends**

  Freshly cut hair has a sharp edge - this tends to get rounder as time goes by; eyelashes taper rapidly.

- **Medulla**

  Human medulla is $< \frac{1}{3}$ of the diameter; animal medulla is $> \frac{1}{2}$ of the diameter.

- **Ovoid bodies**

  Vary between individuals.

- **Cross section (human)**

  Beard hair is triangular; hair from other parts of the head is round; armpit hair is oval; pubic hair varies in diameter and is kinked.

cuticle
cortex
medulla
ovoid body
pigment granule (melanin)

Collection of hairs

Hairs can be collected from a crime scene by picking them up with gloved fingers or clean forceps. Use of different types of lighting and a magnifying glass can make them easier to see. Sometimes sticky tape is used to lift samples from an area in a crime scene or from a garment from a suspect (though the adhesive may interfere with later chemical analysis). Finally a special forensic vacuum cleaner is used to pick up remaining loose material, which can also include other trace evidence, such as glass or paint fragments. All samples are sealed into packets and carefully labelled.

Comparison of hairs

A light microscope is needed to be able to see the detailed structure of hair. Hairs from the crime scene and hairs from suspects are mounted on separate slides. A **comparison microscope** can be used to view two slides simultaneously, making comparisons easy.

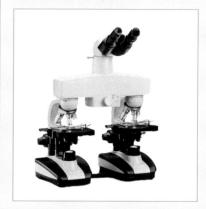

The FBI Handbook of Forensic science states:

'*Hair examinations can determine whether hairs are animal or human. Race, body area, method of removal, damage and alteration (e.g. bleaching or dyeing) can be determined from human hair analysis. Examinations can associate a hair to a person on the basis of microscopic characteristics in the hair but cannot provide absolute personal identification.*'

Fingerprints

The inside surfaces at the ends of your fingers (and toes) are not smooth, but covered by tiny ridges that enhance grip and give you your characteristic fingerprints.

Fingerprints are important as evidence because they are:

- unique - no two fingerprints are alike
- can be classified by pattern
- remain unchanged throughout life.

> The American gangster John Dillinger tried to have his fingerprints removed with acid. Despite all the agony, they grew back and fingerprints were used to confirm his identity in the mortuary, after he had been shot dead by the police.

Classifying fingerprints

Without a system of classification, fingerprints can only be matched by direct comparison. A fingerprint from a crime scene would have to be compared with every fingerprint on file. In 1685, Malpighi named fingerprints as loops or whorls. 200 years later Galton identified arches. These three patterns give the initial basis for fingerprint matching:

- arches rise in the centre (5% of all fingerprints)
- loops double back on themselves (60%)
- whorls form circular patterns (35%)

Further subdivisions are possible: arches may be plain or tented with a sharp central rise. Loops may come up from the thumb or little finger side. Whorls may be plain (concentric circles), pocketed (a loop with a whorl in its end), double loops (wrap around each other) or irregular (a mixture).

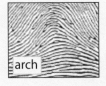 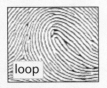 

arch   loop   whorl

Systematic fingerprinting and record keeping started in Argentina in 1891. Five years later, Sir Edward Henry devised a *10-print* system which gave whorls a numerical value according to the fingers that they occurred on. This gave 1024 different codes for sets of fingerprints.

Short *ridges* and *dots* can also be noted, along with enclosed areas or *lakes*. A dot is a very short ridge that looks like a *dot*.

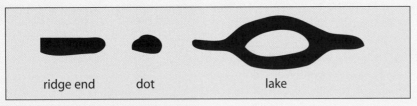

ridge end   dot   lake

Collection of fingerprints

Fingerprints may be **visible** or **latent**.

Visible prints can be made by paint or blood on the fingers, or on a soft surface like putty. These can be photographed and the object they are on is collected as evidence.

Latent prints left by oils and sweat on the skin need to be made visible, then photographed or *lifted* to remove them.

Different methods can be used depending on the type of surface involved:

- **Non- porous surfaces:** Dusting uses powders that stick to the print. The colour of the powder is chosen to contrast with the surface.
- **Porous surfaces:** Powders will clog and the fingerprint tends to soak in and is no longer sticky, so a chemical reagent is used. This reacts with substances in the print. For example, ninhydrin reacts with amino acids in sweat.

A simple torch held at an angle to a fingerprint can make it more visible. Laser or ultraviolet light causes fingerprints to fluoresce (glow) so they can be found and photographed. Fingerprints can also be *fixed* using vapours from heated superglue (cyanoacrylate). The print makes the glue solidify. Modern portable devices use a fluorescent dye mixed with the glue. Using special techniques like this, fingerprints can even be obtained from skin up to 12 hours after an assault.

Matching fingerprints

Traditionally, fingerprints are recorded by inking fingers and rolling them on a card. From the 1960s automated fingerprint identification systems (AFIS) were developed. Nowadays, digital scanning is being used to add prints directly to an electronic database. Computerised systems plot the relative positions of individual ridge characteristics. Shortlists of most likely matches from the national database (NAFIS) to crime scene prints are produced. Expert fingerprint examiners finish the matching process. Up until 1999 the old English system required 16 matching points as evidence that two fingerprints matched exclusively. At the present time, English courts hear expert opinion on the likelihood of two prints matching uniquely.

Body fluids

Blood, saliva, semen or other body fluids such as urine can link a suspect to a crime scene, victim or weapon.

Often, enough good quality DNA can be found for DNA profiling to give a virtually unique match. But there are many other tests that may be carried out by the forensic serologist.

Although these tests may not be as precise as DNA profiling, they can be valuable in establishing a chain of evidence that reveals the events of the crime and establishes the guilt of the perpetrator.

Testing blood

If a stain looks as though it might be blood, the three important questions to answer are:

- Is it blood?
- Is it human blood?
- Who did the blood come from?

Is it blood?

Many stains look like blood. Some simple tests rely on enzymes found in the blood. A common test is to spray an area with **luminol**, which reacts in the presence of the enzyme peroxidase to make blood stains fluoresce (glow in the dark). As only tiny amounts of enzyme are necessary to cause reactions, this is a very sensitive test which will reveal traces of blood even after a criminal has tried to scrub them away. It is a **presumptive test** because other substances can also give a positive result.

Is it human blood?

In 1901, Paul Uhlenhuth injected human cells into a rabbit. The rabbit's immune system made antibodies which reacted with antigens found only in human blood to give a cloudy deposit called precipitin. Today, serologists use synthetic monoclonal antibodies in a kit that can be used in the field.

Who did the blood come from?

There are about 100 antigens found in human blood that occur in different combinations. The most commonly used test is for two antigens, A and B. These may or may not be present in the blood to give four blood groups: A, B, AB (both antigens) or O (neither antigen). Antibody anti-A will react with blood group A or AB, causing the red cells to clump together (**agglutinate**). Similarly, anti B agglutinates group B or AB, but neither antibody affects group O. Testing with antibodies is called **immunoassay**.

		blood group			
		A	B	AB	O
antibody	anti-A	agglutimates	no change	agglutimates	no change
	anti-B	no change	agglutimates	agglutimates	no change

Presumptive tests

A presumptive test allows you to make a **presumption** without being sure.

Presumptive tests are quick, easy and cheap. They establish whether or not more conclusive, demanding and expensive tests are needed.

For example, if a stain is found at a crime scene, a simple test can be carried out to decide if the stain is *likely to be blood*.

If it is, then it can be sent for further analysis, such as DNA profiling.

ABO blood testing

Blood types A and O are very common. The UK averages for each blood type are approximately:

blood type	percentage
O	44
A	42
B	10
AB	4

ABO tests can't pin down an individual, but they're quick and cheap. If you can eliminate suspects whose blood *does not* match crime scene samples, you can save time and resources on further and more expensive investigations.

Collection of blood and body fluids

The position of bloodstains and the patterns formed by them can provide vital evidence about the nature of the crime. So, it's essential to fully document the scene before removing suspected blood samples for analysis. Points to note:

- Health and safety - wear protective clothing (gloves, masks and/or eye protection).

    Wet or moist evidence can be removed in clean plastic containers, **but** growth of microorganisms can destroy or alter moist evidence:

    - samples must be protected from heat and humidity
    - refrigerate as soon as possible
    - remove and air dry completely within two hours and repackage in clean dry paper.

- If possible, remove the entire bloodstained item. If too large choose from:
    - cut away portions
    - scrape into packet
    - tape, lift and stick on acetate
    - absorb onto clean cotton moistened with distilled or deionised water.

- If the stain is not visible, Luminol is a presumptive test only and makes further analysis difficult.

Is the stain semen?

In a rape case, it may be necessary to confirm that a swab or stain contains semen.

At the scene, moistened filter paper can be used to pick up a small amount of fluid for a presumptive test.

If reagents including fast blue B dye are added, a purple colour indicates the presence of SAP (seminal acid phosphate) found in semen.

In the lab, a microscope is used to confirm the presence of sperm.

If no sperm are found, this may be because the rapist has had a vasectomy or is sterile.

An immunoassay test for a protein, P30, is used to confirm that semen is present.

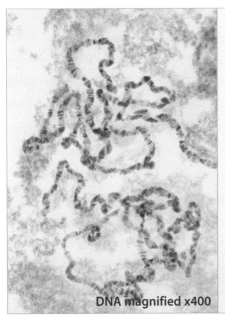

DNA magnified x400

Evidence from DNA

Body fluids (such as blood, semen or saliva) and hair roots can be good sources of DNA for **DNA profiling**. This is often called *DNA fingerprinting*, but some experts don't like the term because your DNA profile isn't unique like a fingerprint. Although everyone (except identical twins) has a unique DNA code, the profiling analysis only uses certain parts of the DNA structure.

DNA profiling uses of a lot of complicated words, so scientists often use abbreviations (like DNA instead of *deoxyribonucleic acid*).

Other terms include:

- **PCR** is the process that *amplifies* a small DNA sample into a large one.
- **Restriction enzymes** cut DNA into pieces.
- **RFLPs** are pieces cut from a DNA molecule.
- **STRs** are small pieces of DNA.
- **Electrophoresis** is the process that separates DNA pieces.
- **SGM+** is the name of the system used to profile DNA.

Wildlife DNA Services is a company in North Wales that specialise in the forensics of wildlife crime. The illegal trafficking of animals and plants is a multi-billion pound industry. Ill-treatment of domestic and wild animals persists in all countries. WDNAS use DNA bloodstain and hair analysis in cases such as:

- smuggling of illegal animal products like shahtoosh (made from the hides of Tibetan antelope)
- badger baiting
- illegal dog fighting
- deer poaching
- identification of unusual species from hairs found at the scene of human crimes
- individual identification of golden eagles, goshawks, merlins, peregrine falcons, gyr falcons and saker falcons
- identification of illegal wild meat entering the UK
- recovery of DNA from dried snake venom for accurate species identification.

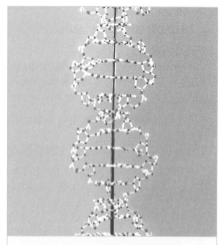

Important facts of DNA profiling ...

DNA is

- found in the nuclei of cells (so not in red blood cells)
- the molecule which forms the genetic code
- made using four different bases (A, T, G, C - short for adenine, thymine, guanine and cytosine) in a definite sequence
- found in the nucleus of cells
- a *double helix* of paired bases (A with T and G with C)
- able to unzip base pairs and make copies of itself by adding new bases.

PCR (polymerase chain reaction)

- uses an enzyme (polymerase) to make DNA copy itself
- can convert tiny amounts of DNA into larger amounts for profiling.

SGM+ (Second Generation Multiplex Plus) is

- the name of the system used since 1998 for the National DNA Database (NDNAD) in the UK
- uses 10 areas (plus a sex indicating area) to give an average uniqueness of the DNA profile of 1 in a billion
- being used to solve crimes committed many years ago
- being used to prove the innocence of wrongly imprisoned people.

DNA extraction

DNA for analysis must be separated from the other cell components.

A detergent and protein digesting enzyme can be used to dissolve cell and nuclear membranes to release the DNA.

This is then extracted using an organic solvent such as ethanol. Modern techniques, e.g. the Qiagen Biorobot EZ1, are automated and very fast.

They use solid extraction systems such as silica beads.

RFLPs, PCR and STRs

Restriction Fragment Length Polymorphism (RFLP or *riflip*) analysis was a method used in the 1980s to make DNA profiles.

Restriction enzymes were used to cut DNA into fragments (the RFLPs) containing repeating base pairs.

A process called *gel electrophoresis* was then used to separate fragments of different lengths to give something that resembled a bar code.

This test needed relatively large samples of DNA.

Many parts of our DNA molecules contain short base sequences (2-5 base pairs) that repeat themselves end to end. These are called *Short Tandem Repeats* or STRs.

From the 1990s, PCR (Polymerase Chain Reaction) has been used to make amplified samples of STRs for DNA profiling.

In a routine DNA analysis, a few nanograms of blood from a crime scene can be amplified to give a complete DNA profile. That's about one forty millionth of a drop!

DNA Low Copy Number (DNA LCN) is a refinement of the SGM+ technique that allows even minute traces of DNA to be used successfully.

For example, a single cell containing less than 10 picograms of DNA can be enough.

Forensic scientists have been able to use cells left in fingerprints on tools, weapons and even matchsticks.

In PCR ...

DNA for analysis is added to a mixture of polymerase enzyme, bases and primers.

Primers are short pieces of DNA that attach to the positions of STRs.

Polymerase causes new short strands of DNA to form between primers.

Repeating the process can amplify the DNA sample by millions of times.

Capillary electrophoresis

The DNA fragments are separated and identified using capillary electrophoresis. Negatively charged DNA is attracted to a positive pole. Modern systems use a narrow capillary tube rather than a porous gel to slow down the movement of the fragments. DNA separates according to size: larger particles move more slowly than the smaller ones.

The primers used in PCR are coloured with fluorescent dyes, so the dyes become attached to the DNA fragments. A laser beam makes each fragment fluoresce when the colour sensitive detector passes it. The flashes of light are recorded as peaks on a chart. These are used to give a DNA profile, which is 20 numbers and gender. The chance of you having the same number code as another person is one in a billion.

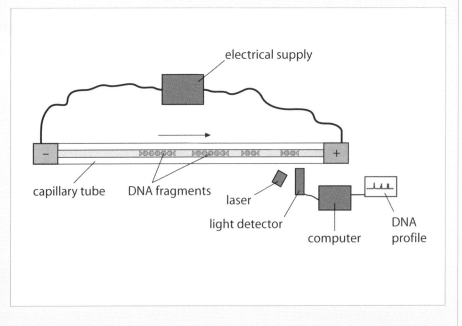

SGM (Second Generation Multiplex) was the DNA profiling system set up in 1995 in the UK. *Multiplex* just means that PCR is used to amplify different pieces of DNA at the same time. SGM used six STR markers and a sex indicating marker. Since 1998, SGM+ has been used. It tests 10 STRs along with sex. This has made possible the analysis of mixed DNA samples, common in rape cases.

The UK National DNA Database (NDNAD) now contains more than three million profiles.

INSECTS, TEETH AND BONES

Clues from insects

Experts who study *bugs* for legal purposes are called **forensic entomologists**. Originally insects were used to provide estimates of the time of death, but they can be used to track the times and locations of many other events.

For example:

- drug hauls can be inspected for insects for evidence of the country of origin
- routes taken by stolen cars can be determined from the remains of dead insects stuck to them.

How long has the body been there?

Insect life cycles can be used to estimate the time since death. They progress from eggs to larvae to adults. As insects have exoskeletons, they have to shed their skins to grow. This means that different larval stages, called **instars**, can be recognised. The changes are called **metamorphosis** and may be *complete* or *incomplete*:

- **Complete** - insects like beetles and flies have a final larval stage which turns into a pupa, from which a completely different adult form emerges.
- **Incomplete** - insects like locusts show a gradual transformation to adult form at each stage.

Of the millions of insect species, only a few hundred are attracted to decaying corpses. Of these, the most useful is probably the blowfly. The larva sheds its skin twice before pupating.

How do scientists know how long each stage takes? One of the first *CSI* programmes featured a character called Grissom who collected insects, measured temperatures, raised larvae and waited for the adults to emerge. Kept at a constant 21 °C, the blowfly life cycle takes 345 hours.

If night temperatures are lower, the actual life cycle will be longer and forensic entomologists will need to take the previous local weather conditions into account.

Further clues are given by the fact that different insect species tend to arrive at different times as the corpse decays. Taken with a study of the state of decay, if time since death is three weeks or less, it can be estimated to within a day or two. The five main stages of body tissue breakdown are shown in the table.

days after death	stage	description	insects
0-3	initial decay	external appearance shows only small changes	blowflies
4-7	putrefaction	bacteria cause the skin to gain a greenish tint which spreads outwards from the abdomen; veins near the surface become more visible; gases produced by microorganisms cause the body to swell and smell	fly larvae and beetles which feed on them
8-18	black putrefaction	flesh discolours and may be blue, green, purple, brown or black; the swelling collapses as gases escape; tissues become fluid; smell increases; intestines decay first followed by liver, lungs, brain and the kidneys; stomach decay may be delayed if it is full of acid	ants, cockroaches and beetles
19-30	butyric putrefaction	fluids escape and the body dries out; usually covered by mould; odour changes and becomes less vile	as parts of the body dry out different species are attracted to the different wet and dry parts
31+	dry decay	tissues dry out and rot away until only bones, teeth and hair remain	beetles and clothes moth larvae (feed on hair)

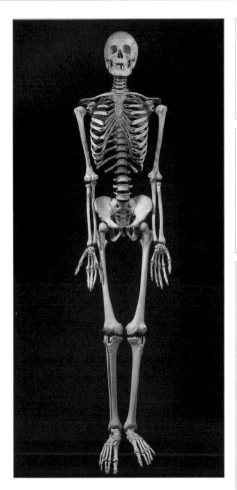

Clues from bodies

How do forensic scientists know

- the rate of decay of bodies in different conditions
- which insects are found at different stages?

These and other questions are answered at the *body farm* in Tennessee. Its correct name is the University of Tennessee Forensic Anthropology Facility. Here, bodies donated to science are buried in graves at different depths, left in the open on the ground covered by leaves or tied upright against tree trunks. Long term studies are being carried out to determine exactly what happens to human bodies after death.

Since the 1970s, William Bass, a **forensic anthropologist**, has been studying the rate and pattern of decay under a wide range of conditions. His team are investigating and devising more accurate methods for determining the time of death and better body locating techniques, including ground penetrating radar. The FBI regularly call on his expertise.

The bare bones

Skeletons reveal a lot of information - even a single bone or tooth can be useful. If teeth are present, a **forensic odontologist** will help.

Investigators try to answer these questions to develop a profile of the victim:

Are the bones human?

Some animal bones resemble human bones, for example sheep and deer ribs are like human ribs and horse tail bones are like human finger bones.

How old is the victim?

Teeth are especially helpful. Teeth develop from the appearance and loss of the 20 milk teeth by age 12. Up to 32 permanent teeth develop by age 18, when wisdom teeth may appear. In adults, the wear patterns of teeth and a progressive lightening of the roots from the base upwards can be taken into account.

Bones become denser and larger as children develop. A process of **ossification** takes place, with cartilage being replaced by bone as bones fuse together. There are 800 centres of ossification that can be used to estimate age. The collarbone is the last bone to finish growing, at up to age 28.

What sex is the victim?

Male skulls have a ridge above the eyes. There is also prominent bone below the ears and at the bottom of the back of the skull where muscles attach. The female pelvis is wider and with a larger cavity for childbirth. Without the skull or hips, anthropologists look at the size of areas for muscle attachment, which tend to be larger in men.

What ethnicity is the victim?

Skulls of different ethnic groups have distinctive features. The Asian or Mongoloid skull is tall with a broad, flat face and projecting cheek bones. Afro-Caribbean skulls have a wide nose opening and larger teeth than other groups. The cranium is long. Caucasians have skulls which are high and wide. Cheek bones and jaw do not project. The jaw falls behind a vertical line from the forehead.

How tall is the victim?

A complete skeleton can be assembled and 10-11 cm is added to make up for the missing soft tissues. More is added for children according to age. Height can also be calculated from the length of other bones.

Are there any distinctive features?

Bones become thicker with use. So right or left handedness and features associated with work habits are assessed. Bones may have been damaged by diseases or injury. Surgical appliances such as artificial hips may be present.

What's the cause of death?

Bullets may leave holes; sharp weapons may cut or chip bones. Unhealed fractures also indicate violence.

What do they look like?

If the skull is available and other evidence hasn't helped to identify the victim, facial reconstruction may be attempted. The bones determine the size and shape of the muscles that attach to them. The shape of the face can be approximated by working out the muscle distribution. This can be done by drawing, attaching clay to a cast of the skull or using computer programmes. Eye colour, structure of the eyelids and the nose and the colour and style of the hair have to be a *best guess*. Nonetheless, many facial reconstructions have successfully led to eventual identification.

Dental records and DNA

Anthropologists and odontologists often have to help to identify victims of mass disasters, such as earthquakes, flooding or air crashes.

In such cases they may have a list of names to work with. Whenever there are possible candidates to match to remains, the experts can try to obtain data to confirm identification. If DNA can be obtained, it can be matched with samples from relatives.

Each individual shares half their DNA with their parents or children. Such tests are expensive and time-consuming, so dental records are especially useful if they are available. Features used to make matches include:

- shape of mouth arch

- misalignment of teeth

- width of teeth

- spacing of teeth

- missing teeth

- wear patterns.

Bite marks

In violent crimes, victims are sometimes bitten by the assailant.

Sometimes, criminals leave partly-eaten food at the scene of a crime.

Forensic scientists have to be alert and collect such evidence at the earliest opportunity - bite marks in flesh fade, and food decays.

Bite marks can be matched to dental records using computer matching techniques or by laying acetate diagrams of the suspect's teeth over a wound.

In one assault case, the suspect alleged that the victim had bitten him. But the odontologist was able to show that he had bitten himself! In such cases the odontologist has to act as an expert witness in court.

For identification purposes, dental records must be full and accurate. Unfortunately this is not always the case ...

In 1985, a body was exhumed in Brazil. It was believed to be the notorious Josef Mengele - Hitler's *angel of death* - who oversaw the deaths of 400 000 people.

Mengele's Nazi SS file contained a 1938 dental chart. But this just showed that he had 12 fillings, without detailing which teeth were affected. Richard Helmar, a German forensic anthropologist used a photograph of the skull to mark 30 identification points. He then superimposed a photograph of Mengele over the skull photo and decided that there was a perfect match.

In 1992 his conclusions were confirmed when DNA from the bones was compared with samples from Mengele's relatives.

Physical evidence

Physical evidence includes:

- marks and impressions such as footprints and tool marks,
- trace evidence such as fibres, glass and paint.

Physical analysis of blood can reveal what took place while a crime was being committed.

Methods of analysis

Chemical analysis is used to identify chemical compounds associated with crimes, such as drugs, explosives and gunshot residues. Some techniques:

- paper, gas, thin layer and column chromatography
- high performance liquid chromatography (HPLC)
- electrophoresis (see section on DNA profiling)
- visible, infrared (IR), ultraviolet (UV)
- mass spectroscopy
- comparison microscopy of crystals
- colorimetry.

Chromatography

This type of analysis can be used to identify many chemicals, including dyes and drugs.

Molecules are moved by a **mobile phase** but slowed down to different extents by a **stationary phase**. In paper and thin layer chromatography a liquid solvent called an eluant (mobile phase) travels along a solid sheet of filter paper or granular material (stationary phase) on a glass or plastic sheet.

Separation of black ink on thin layer chromatography plate.

Image reproduced under the terms of the GNU Free Documentation License

As molecules pass along, even small differences will cause substances to separate into spots of pure chemical that can be analysed. Inks used in forgeries can be compared this way. For example, two different black inks are likely to contain a mixture of different pigments, which will show up when separated.

Gas chromatography and high performance liquid chromatography (HPLC) are in common use in forensic labs.

- Sample for analysis is placed in a vaporiser.
- Vaporised particles are carried through a long tube by an inert gas (mobile phase).
- The tube contains liquid on the sides or on granules (stationary phase).
- The time for each substance to pass along the tube is recorded using a detector at the end of the tube.
- Unknown substances can be recognised by comparing times with known substances.
- Tiny samples can be analysed, but this makes it easy to contaminate.

Visible, UV and IR Spectroscopy

We are used to being able to tell things apart by their colours. Colour depends on which wavelengths of light are reflected or absorbed. A spectrophotometer accurately tests which wavelengths are reflected or absorbed by a chemical, so that it can be identified. Non-visible wavelengths in the infrared and ultraviolet regions of the electromagnetic spectrum can also be used.

Mass spectroscopy

Bombardment with high energy electrons smashes the molecules under test into charged particles (ions). The particles are then accelerated by an electric field and separated by size using a magnetic field. Smaller particles emerge and are detected first. Each chemical has its characteristic *signature* of particles of different sizes.

Toxicology

Forensic toxicologists are concerned with substances that can cause harm to the body. They identify substances found at crime scenes or detect their presence in the body, including:

- illegal drugs, such as heroin and ecstasy (MDMA)
- performance-enhancing drugs used by athletes
- legal drugs, such as aspirin or alcohol
- chemicals used as poisons, such as arsenic or cyanide.

Colorimetry

Colorimetry is used to determine the concentration of a coloured solution. Light is shone through it. The higher the concentration the more light is absorbed. Measuring the amount that passes through tells you the concentration.

Toxicology (continued ...)

In the case of a suspicious death, poisoning may be suspected. Depending on circumstances, the pathologist who carries out the post mortem examination sends samples of body tissues for analysis.

- Stomach contents, liver, kidneys, the brain and urine from the bladder are often sent for further analysis.
- Bile concentrates antidepressants and morphine.
- Volatile substances may show up in the lungs.
- Hair stores a record of poisoning in bands along the length of the hair.
- Arsenic poisoning can be detected when the body has almost entirely decayed as it can be detected in hair, nails and bone.

Blood and urine are useful samples to take from living subjects.

Analysis is often difficult, as substances may be diluted and altered by processes in the body. For example, heroin is very quickly converted into morphine. A drug ingested in milligrams is spread throughout the body so it's present in a sample in micrograms.

Screening for drugs

Simple tests can be carried out before more complex analysis.

substance	test and POSITIVE RESULT
heroin or morphine	methanal and sulfuric acid - PURPLE amphetamine solution - ORANGE-BROWN
barbiturates	dilute cobalt acetate in methanol, add isopropylamine - VIOLET
LSD	acidified dimethylaminobenzaldehyde in ethanol - BLUE-PURPLE
cocaine	• cobalt thiocyanate in water and glycerol - BLUE • add hydrochloric acid - PINK • then chloroform - BLUE IN CHLOROFORM LAYER ONLY

Confirmation

If pure samples can be obtained, the substance may be crystallised.

A comparison microscope can then be used to match the crystals with known substances.

HPLC or thin layer chromatography may be used, depending on what is being tested for. But gas chromatography is one of the most useful tools for the toxicologist attempting to confirm the identity of a substance. A gas chromatograph is often linked to a mass spectrometer (GC/MS) so that chemical composition can be identified and proof provided.

Forensic toxicologists have to carefully record and interpret their analysis, so it can be presented in court to a jury of non-experts.

When Napoleon Bonaparte died, his valet kept a lock of his hair. Tested nearly 180 years later, it showed that he had been poisoned by heavy doses of arsenic administered over a period of four months.

Footprints

Shoe and boot prints are usually called *footprints*, although a bare footprint could have toe prints just like fingerprints. On hard surfaces, footprints of any kind can be developed and lifted like fingerprints. But impressions in soft material like mud can provide greater detail of the original shoe.

Although manufacturers use a wide variety of designs for soles and heels - especially of trainers - they are usually mass produced. But wear causes unique marks to appear.

- databases are used to identify the make and type of shoe
- size and depth of a footprint gives a rough idea of the height and weight of the wearer
- *Treadmark*, a database similar to the NAFIS fingerprint system, is being developed.

You're Niked!

A thief in Torquay stole a *Nike* jacket and escaped through a window. Three weeks later, staff found an old pair of trainers in a shoebox. The thief had swapped them for new ones when he stole the jacket. A scan of the old trainers matched shoes in the *Treadmark* database to a man previously arrested for an unconnected crime.

Collection of footprints

Accurate recording of the impressions is essential if they are to be used as evidence in a court of law.

Enhanced photography with a measuring scale next to the print is used.

But obtaining a cast can record more detail.

- Footprints can be filled with plaster or dental stone.
- Fragile material like sand can first be stabilised with sprays.
- Snow prints can be lifted by spraying with wax and using a chilled casting material.

Simple measurements of features can be used to link a shoe from a suspect with a cast, or distinctive patterns may be copied onto acetate and superimposed onto a shoe for comparison. The Forensic Science Service has developed a database called *Footwear Intelligence Technology* (FIT) available from March 2007, which is:

'designed to help police increase crime detection rates by quickly identifying footwear marks left at crime scenes and linking these to other crimes and suspects.'

Toolmarks

Even if a clever criminal has left no fingerprints, footprints or DNA, they may have used a tool when carrying out their crime. It might be a jemmy to force open a door or break a padlock, or even a weapon used to strike a victim or a saw to cut up a corpse.

Three kinds of mark

The working edge of any tool will often show tiny imperfections caused by use or during manufacture. These will show up in the marks left on surfaces.

- **Indentations** occur when a tool is pressed into softer material such as wood, vinyl or a metal like aluminium. The type of tool may be identified, e.g. a screwdriver of a particular size.

- **Sliding marks** are made when a tool slides or scratches across a surface. A characteristic pattern of lines may be left due to imperfections in the edge of the tool.

- **Cutting marks** are left by tools like bolt cutters or pliers, which leave characteristic marks, especially if the tool has been frequently sharpened.

The microscopic lines (known as *striations*) made by a tool under controlled conditions can be compared with marks left at the scene of the crime - another job for the comparison microscope.

Collection of toolmarks

If possible, useful marks are removed from the scene, for example, a forced window frame or the damaged part of it.

Carefully-lit photographs are taken to enhance the visibility of features.

Resin or rubberised silicone sealant can be used to make casts. These can record microscopic detail that plaster used for a footprint would fail to distinguish.

Fibres, glass and paint fragments

According to the *exchange theory*, criminals always leave and take away traces at the scene of a crime.

Fibres, glass and paint fragments can all be used to link the criminal and the crime.

Collection of trace evidence

Skill and patience are required when searching for trace evidence. Particles must be collected carefully and wrapped separately to prevent cross contamination. Smaller items can be packed and sealed in clean paper using pharmacy folds (bindles) and placed in envelopes. Labels, photographs and sketches are used to record where the contents have come from.

- Larger fragments are picked up using gloved hands or forceps.
- In small areas, adhesive tape can be used to lift and remove traces.
- Portable objects can be bagged and removed for scraping and washing in the lab.
- Finally, forensic vacuum cleaners suck particles onto filter paper or into clean bags.

Laboratory analysis

Back in the laboratory, microscopes can reveal special features of fragments that can't be seen by the naked eye.

A wide variety of other analytical techniques is available to characterise samples. These range from simple burning tests, to identification of chemical compounds using sophisticated techniques, such as chromatography and mass spectroscopy.

Fibres

Fibres are easily shed or picked up. There are many different types.

- They vary in cross-sectional shape.
- Animal fibres such as wool are hairs which therefore have characteristic scales.
- Plant species have unique fibres that identify them, e.g. cotton has twisted ribbon-like fibres, linen (flax) fibres are tube-like and pointed at the ends.
- Initial analysis can be done by investigating the burning properties of fibres.
- Synthetic fibres can be investigated by looking at their solubility in solvents and melting points.
- Dyes in fibres can be extracted for thin layer chromatography or microspectrophotometry.

Paint

Paint fragments can be exchanged in car accidents and when burglars use tools. Paint varies in colour (pigments) and other chemical components, e.g. as in car paints and house paints.

- Paint fragments seldom contain a single layer. If several layers in two samples match, the link is very unlikely to be by chance.
- Paint sample edges can be cut and polished to make the colour sequence clearer.
- Microspectrophotometry makes it possible to compare graphs of wavelengths emitted and absorbed for tiny paint chips. In matching samples the characteristic peaks coincide.
- Make and model of car may be revealed by paint chips left at an accident scene.

Glass

Windows are often broken in burglaries. Car headlights are often broken in car accidents. Spectacles, bottles and glasses can be broken in a variety of circumstances.

There are many different types of glass manufactured for different purposes. Useful properties for comparison are:

- colour
- density
- refractive index.

> A man in Iowa gave himself up when he heard the police were looking for a Toyota Corolla. He assumed there had been a witness - but actually, forensic scientists had used glass fragments to identify the vehicle model and make.

Blood splatters

Bloodstains can reveal an amazing amount of detail about a crime.

Size, shape and position can reveal where the attacker was standing, how many blows they struck, whether they were right- or left-handed and how tall they were.

The pattern formed by a drop of blood when it strikes a surface depends on size, direction and force. For example:

- blood dripping a short vertical distance will form circles
- large drops flung at an angle will break into smaller drops and splash into elongated tails which point away from the direction they came.

Separate patterns will point back towards the original source, so the position of the assailant and victim in a room at the moment of the attack can be estimated. Originally, the path of the drops was assumed to be straight. Computer simulations now allow for the effect of gravity in creating a gentle curve.

Blood flung from the edge or tip of a weapon will travel in a curve to left or right depending on which hand was used. The width of the track of blood from a knife is narrower than from a blunt instrument such as a pickaxe handle. The number of trails would indicate the number of blows and the splatters would show how forceful they were. Evidence of a ferocious attack would be evidence against a plea of self-defence.

A *shadow* area without blood would suggest that something has been moved. A bag taken away by the attacker could show marks which fit neatly into the rest of the pattern. A smear suggests that the attacker has something that has blood on it. Blood splatters only occur at the time of the incident, so blood splatter patterns on the clothes or body put a suspect at the scene at the time of the attack.

Detailed photography is needed to record all aspects of bloods splatter, using wide angle shots of the overall patterns and close-ups with scales to reveal size.